Keep Walking

Leadership Learning in Action

Alan Chambers MBE

&

Dr Richard Hale

ISBN 9781904312789

MX Publishing

335 Princess Park Manor, Royal Drive, London, N11 3GX

www.mxpublishing.co.uk

To

Richard Mark Bell

The bravest man I ever knew, who faced immense daily adversity and frustration and never complained

Alan

Oliver & William

'Keep walking boys'

Dad

About the Authors

Alan Chambers MBE, led the first successful unassisted attempt to reach the Geographic North Pole from Canada in 2000. Unassisted means having no external help and support along the way. No food caches, dog teams, air re-supplies, over-snow vehicles, or relay teams.

This followed what he referred to as his 'successful failure', the attempt to do the same in 1998 when he had to be rescued from treacherous circumstances. Following this experience, when many others would have given up, Alan planned and researched meticulously, living for months at a time with the Inuit communities in Northern Canada.

He recruited for the Team Polar 2000 expedition, organized sponsorship, trained the team and led them on the ice. He and Charlie Paton, who had never skied before, were the two members of the party to reach the Pole having travelled 472 nautical miles dragging 250 pounds of stores each, the weight of a baby elephant. On the journey they faced incredible adversity, including being isolated on an ice flow where they drifted 400 nautical miles. After 70 days manhauling under the worst conditions in the world, Team Polar 2000 reached the Geographical North Pole at 23:46 hrs on the 16th May 2000.

Alan earned a place in the history books in the great tradition of Polar exploration and was awarded the MBE for 'outstanding leadership in the face of extreme adversity.'

Since then Alan has worked with major global corporations telling the story of his adventure, and conveying key lessons of leadership.

Alan has a vision for a new of model of leadership which transcends the world of exploration to the world of business. He takes business leaders to Arctic and Antarctic having led several trips to the geographic North Pole and in January 2009 to the South Pole, to support their personal development. He works with Richard Hale supporting action learning based programmes of leadership development in business, inspirational presentations and personal coaching and mentoring.

Dr Richard Hale, has worked for the past 25 years in the field of corporate management and leadership development. His early career was spent with GEC and BSkyB where he headed management development and training functions. He has written several books related to leadership development and is author of the renowned *Impact and Influence* resources which support personal development. Richard researched the subject of mentoring for his doctorate and has a passion for work based learning – enabling leaders to learn from their experience.

This is based on action learning principles and has been used in major international corporations such as Lloyds TSB, HBOS, Pfizer, FleetPartners, EDF Energy and the Virgin group.. Richard works closely with universities which accredit his work based learning questions process enabling business leaders to achieve qualifications at postgraduate level based on their work in business. He has also applied this methodology to the Continuing Professional Development of accountants and Human Resource professionals and is active in developing the professional development pathway for professional in the field of outourcing.

Richard and Alan deliver leadership workshops, inspirational presentations and education programmes for corporate organizations and personal coaching and mentoring. They can be contacted at:

richard@adventurousbusiness.com

Associated websites:

www.adventruousbusiness..com

www.keepwalkinglearning.com

www.alan-chambers.com

www.richardhaleassociates.com

www.feetofgreen.com

Contents

1 - What Does Leadership Mean to You?

By Richard Hale

How did I get here? And where am I going? These are two key questions I ask leaders who join our leadership development programmes to consider. Simple questions but ones which force self-reflection. In corporate organizations many leaders find themselves in positions of leadership without having necessarily embarked on a career intending to be a leader. They may have achieved upward progress in their professional role which has eventually taken them to a position where they have to lead others. Some are reluctant leaders and when they properly address these questions they realize that leadership is not for them. Conversely, some people discover they had a latent ability as a leader and they emerge as an influential leader once they are offered, and take, the opportunity.

What does leadership mean to me? What sort of a leader am I? Two simple questions; but essential for anyone to be able to answer with conviction who claims to be a leader, or holds the title. I find it fascinating that in many of the leadership development programmes we run, people join the programme and begin by thinking leadership is a subject to be studied, more than lived. So, we will often have debates about whether leaders are born or made or discuss the traits of effective leaders. It is as though leadership is an objective subject which can be defined, studied and analyzed. It is as though these people with the title leader, do not see themselves as real leaders; the real leaders in their eyes are the great world leaders or business leaders, such as Nelson Mandela, Winston Churchill, Mahatma Gandhi, Jack Welch or Richard Branson. I don't see it like this. I believe there is evidence of effective and ineffective leadership at all levels of organization around us, and it worthy of study, because the context is often more closely aligned with our own reality.

Then there are government and corporate organizations that seek to define leadership. Often this is based on a well intentioned desire to control leadership and to define the key leadership capabilities that are required. Sadly, though, this can lead to an over emphasis on analysis and assessment, which stymies action; a kind of analysis paralysis.

I believe that leadership is not an academic subject that benefits much from objective study. It is a practical subject that is as much about subjective experience.

Indeed, it is situational, as one style does not fit all situations, but to reduce it to one model of situational leadership is to over simplify it. Equally, not every style of leadership fits every personality. Some leaders may be very effective and comfortable with a quiet, persuasive style, whereas others are more suited to an inspirational motivational style.

A key competence that has recently been identified with the growth of interest in emotional intelligence is that of 'authenticity'. I do think that the most effective leaders are authentic. They are 'comfortable in their own skin', as I recall one senior leader in global banking saying.

Let me describe a conference I attended which was positioned as a summit of key leaders brought together from different sectors such as business, education and academia. I was invited to join this conference as a guest and arrived in good spirits and keen to learn about the experiences of leaders and to find out how others who were involved in developing leaders were doing it. A string of speakers stood up, including erudite business school professors, and gave a series of thirty to forty minute presentations. What were the common messages about leadership from all the research.

- Leadership should be developed through Socratic methods, by encouraging the asking of questions.
- Leaders should be encouraged to gain significant learning through experience.
- Effective leaders engage with those they seek to lead and gain commitment through involvement.
- Leadership is about daring to be different.

I sat in the audience agreeing with all these points, for they echoed my own experience, whether seeking to develop leadership in the corporate world or whether trying to demonstrate leadership personally in the business world.

Yet as I sat there listening to those billed as experts in leadership I started to feel a niggling unease. If the presenters and the audience were all interested in leadership, and most were in some sense leaders themselves, why was it that they seemed to be incapable of following the findings from the research?

I was itching to ask questions but the audience was not allowed to ask a question until two and half hours into the programme. Then questions were strictly controlled by the Chair, who perhaps saw his leadership role as one of controller.

I looked around the room and guessed about the experience in the audience, and how it significantly outweighed that of the formal speakers. I became agitated that I was not getting to hear about the real life experiences of these leaders.

Then I thought about the concept of involvement and engagement. We were mostly sat in tiered rows in a traditional lecture theatre style room, staring at the back of the head of the person in front. Apart from the experts; they had a position on stage or at the dais. So how were we meant to achieve involvement with one another?

Then I thought about the idea of daring to be different and I realized, we were working to the traditional model, the expected approach for running a conference. There was no way we were going to dare to be different.

It was as though we should listen to the 'objective and scientific' findings about leadership as though it was something 'out there', but we were behaving in the absolutely opposite way; no questions, no sharing of experience, no involvement and no daring to be different. Admittedly, I did not disrupt the system; I like everyone else in the room played along. It seemed there was a collective 'groupthink' thing going on. When I asked other people individually over coffee about this, they agreed that the format should be different, but nobody dared to speak out publicly. That would have meant really daring to be different, non conformist, revolutionary even. We were, I felt, a bunch of hypocrites.

I had for some years been thinking that the traditional conference model had become tired. I think this was related to the fact that I had become increasingly committed to an action learning based approach to leadership development. I had been influenced by the thinking of Professor Reg Revans, the founding father of action learning. Action learning is, simply put, a belief that leaders learn best with and from others in a social way. What I did propose to the conference organizer was that we might be involved in supporting a different style of conference to be run in the future, one which started with the participants coming along and sharing their questions and issues, and then working with each other to decide on actions they could take. As an approach this sounds simplistic and obvious, but as Revans himself said, 'action learning is so simple a concept it took the business schools a full forty years to misunderstand it.' Thankfully the conference organization was receptive, and was willing to dare to be different.

My view is that leaders would be better off sharing leadership experiences and practices and deciding what action to take in their own reality, rather than focusing on the ideal traits or competencies to develop. If they work on a real world challenge, and can in the process learn from similar experiences or draw on the ideas of others, then they will have to demonstrate many of the competencies of leadership. Organizations and those concerned with the development of leaders have become too obsessed with measurement, often against a proclaimed normative model of 'effective leadership'. This has led to too much assessment and not enough action.

One might ask the question what lies behind this search for the ideal model of leadership. It is not just that we run conferences on the subject of leadership. There is an industry in leadership books, and the psychologists have created a business in competency profiling, assessment and development centres, and consultants have emerged as the developers of individual leaders. Succession planning and talent management have become part of everyday organizational parlance as we seek to create the best, the ideal leader. An organizational psychologist friend of mine, Malcolm Ballantine, recognizes the challenges. He realized part way through running a senior level government assessment centre, intended to identify and select top leaders for the future, that the process of testing against a set of precisely defined competencies was set up in such a way that the organizers might as well have said to the participating leaders, 'For this job we are looking for superman or superwoman, but unfortunately we have got you.'

Whilst we might idealize the great world leaders or charismatic business leaders, this is perhaps driven by our optimism, our hope that there is a perfect model leader; if we keep looking perhaps we will find the right one. In some cases I would argue that we idealize the leader because it creates a convenient psychological relationship of dependency. It is as though the follower says, 'Well the institution has made this person the leader, who must know what is right and is a better person than me. As I am powerless there is no point in questioning how things are done. I will play the game as I depend on the institution and the leader for my livelihood and my future.'

Psychologists called this 'learned helplessness', and sadly despite all the advances in technologies and human capabilities, it is alive and well in the corporation of the twenty-first century.

In reality all leaders are blessed or cursed with the human condition. When we are seeking to be led, we are prone to idealize our leaders. We focus on their strengths, and turn a blind eye to weaknesses or rationalize, finding excuses on their behalf. Surely history and literature from Greek tragedy to Shakespeare has taught us though that often as not, power corrupts and 'hubris' precedes 'nemesis'. And once the tide of feeling turns against a leader who is falling out of favour and the crowd senses it acceptable to speak out, then we see the coup.

Witness the rapid exit of Margaret Thatcher from government in 1990. Her political demise was one of the most dramatic episodes in British political history. The idea that such a long-serving prime minister, who had been undefeated at the polls should could be removed by an internal party ballot seemed most unlikely. However, on 1 November 1990, Sir Geoffrey Howe, one of Thatcher's greatest supporters, resigned as Deputy Prime Minister in protest at her European policy and suggested that the time had come for 'others to consider their own response to the tragic conflict of loyalties'. Michael Heseltine, her former Cabinet colleague, then challenged her for the leadership of the party, and attracted sufficient support in the first round of voting to prolong the contest to a second ballot. Though she initially stated that she intended to contest the second ballot, Thatcher decided, after consulting with her Cabinet colleagues, to withdraw from the contest. On 22 November she announced to the Cabinet that she would not be a candidate in the second ballot.

My own interest in leadership and in particular the development of leadership within organizations is driven partly by this fascination with the fact that leadership is not a science. It has existed as a concept since man and in truth, whilst some 'authorities' might claim to have found the answer in terms of how to define it, assess it or develop it, 'it' remains something of a mystery. I tend towards a view that psychologists would call 'social constructionist', that is that leadership is a concept we as humans have constructed in our own minds to help us try to understand it. There is no one formula that can be applied in terms of leadership in every situation. Human judgement plays a significant part in determining whether a leader is successful in any given situation. Indeed what one person sees as successful may not be seen in the same way by others. In other words we do not all measure by the same criteria, despite the many attempts by organizations in the current era to agree a normative set of leadership competencies. So one person might view their Chief Executive as a successful leader because of their personal financial achievements, whereas another organization member may view this same leader as weak because they fail to uphold stated organizational values of integrity. In a sense success may be as determined in the eye of the beholder.

It is this messiness about leadership, its situational and ambiguous nature, which I see frustrating the hell out of many of those who see themselves initially as students of leadership on the programmes we run in the corporate world. In time, participants come to realize there is not one truth about leadership. It is situational, there is a need to manage ambiguity, and it is up to you to decide how you define leadership and what sort of leader you want to be. So if leadership is so subjective then what can a book such as this offer? Well, we don't claim to provide the one truth, but we aim to share experiences, and the essence of some of the learning gained over recent years in both leadership development and in acting as leaders.

For many years I have been delivering training programmes to managers and leaders in organizations and I have come to realize I have on occasions been colluding in a game that trainers and participants on courses often play. I would be positioned as the expert on management skills subjects, participants would sit and be entertained by me. I gradually improved my entertaining skills, and the organizations employing me would note with satisfaction that my aggregated scores on the feedback sheets were continuing to rise. We all knew the game; the course organizer would tick the box for training days provided, I would deliver according to my formula and get paid and the participants would enjoy a few days of respite from the real world. I asked myself some serious questions about my own authenticity. I wasn't sure I wanted to continue a career in this mode.

So we asked the question: 'What would Reg say we should do?' We postulated, Reg would say we should start with questions. Leave the theory to follow on once the participants have defined their questions. And so the Leadership Questions approach was created. Since 2000 we have introduced the Leadership Questions approach to several international organizations to support leadership development, including HBOS, Lloyds TSB, Westbury Homes, B&Q, Pfizer and EDF Energy in the UK and several government and public sector organizations. When we conceived of the idea, as with any pioneering approach, there were more people who told us, if not directly, 'It'll never work.'

I am reminded of the parallel with Alan Chambers being given a five percent chance of succeeding in his attempt to reach the North Pole from Canada unassisted. We started to look to educational institutions, universities and professional institutes who would recognize our approach and provide accreditation. It felt at the time like we might have been swimming against the tide. Why would a university that prides itself on managing knowledge, and leading with knowledge input in the design of its programmes, ever want to accredit a programme which has no predetermined input and allows its students to define their own questions? The more I learned about the work of Revans the more I realized he faced the same challenges in his time, his message falling on deaf ears with the educational establishment. Despite the evidence of the benefit of his approach with major industries such the coal industry after nationalization post World War Two, and in the health sector, and his great success in linking higher education with business improvement in Belgium, Revans was seen as too revolutionary in his own land. He had dared to be different.

However, we held to our belief that we were doing the right thing, and we now have three universities in the UK that formally recognize our Leadership Questions process. This provides credits leading to recognized qualifications up to Masters Degree level. In a period of two years Lloyds TSB Asset Finance Division has registered over 40 of its leaders on a Leadership Questions based programme at Masters Level. There are over 350 pieces of evidence of significant action and learning produced by leaders. One of the Leadership Questions alone tackled by a participant, has saved the business over one million pounds sterling per annum. Yet the Managing Director of the division, when told about this, said, 'Great, but it's not just about the money is it? Has there been some real learning?' It was when I heard this that I knew we had turned a significant corner. In the world of management development, the trainers and consultants pain themselves over how to prove benefits at the level of return on investment. Often they concoct phoney formulae to justify their role and contribution, fearful of the line manager or managing director who will challenge them on how their training programmes have benefited the bottom line. So here we were with a Managing Director, of a hard nosed commercial business, recognizing that we should focus on the learning, and then the business benefits would follow.

Bob Collingham, Head of Development Programmes, was willing to back our approach when I first described it to him. Not without personal risk, he dared to be different because he believed we were doing the right thing. The Leadership Questions approach is now being used to support Continuing Professional Development, under the banner of CPD Questions for professionals, in finance and human resource disciplines for instance, and it is recognized by several professional institutions.

It was Bob Collingham who introduced me to Alan Chambers, the polar explorer, because he said he felt we had a common belief in action learning. Alan did not necessarily call it action learning, but there was no doubt in my mind, when I heard about what Alan had achieved, that he was an action learner. He took action and he learned from it. Additionally, he learned from others who had gone before him, as he will describe later in the book.

Furthermore, Alan struck me as an authentic leader. If you were asked to imagine an ex-commando polar explorer you might conjure up stereotyped images of the big, loud, aggressive leader of men. That is not Alan. He is softly spoken, assertive but not aggressive, and you instantly sense when you look him in the eye that he will talk straight with you and he expects you to reciprocate. He doesn't want to be glorified, he hates to be called a hero and you sense he knows himself. However, Alan thinks big, and has achieved big. He wants to contribute to raising the bar for leadership in organizations and his own achievements provide real inspiration to others. The question he asks leaders to consider is:

What legacy do I want to leave behind as a leader?

What you know when he asks other leaders to consider this question, is that he has asked the question of himself. Furthermore, at a relatively young age, he has provided some answers. Who knows what his full legacy will be, but already he has tested himself to create new definitions of what is achievable. He successfully led the first unassisted expedition from Canada to the North Pole in 2000. More men have stood on the moon than have walked to the North Pole. He has received recognition including the honour bestowed by the Queen of becoming a Member of the British Empire (MBE) for 'extraordinary leadership in conditions of extreme adversity.' As a real leader though, Alan is not in it for honours, prizes or fame. He wants to test himself to the limit, and to realize what he can achieve. In doing so he wants to challenge others to raise their game as leaders.

We live in an era when so-called celebrities are writing their autobiographies in their twenties, perhaps having achieved fame and fortune but certainly they are not leaving a legacy. As role models they are creating a false sense amongst their followers that there is a short cut to success, rather than, as is more often the case, a long hard road of adversity and a requirement for hard work combined with ability.

So, Alan and I have joined forces because we believe we have a story to tell, which we will hope will help leaders seeking to develop, and those seeking to help the development of leaders. Alan's expeditions are rich with stories and experiences which provide powerful metaphors for leadership development and learning in business. And as he told me they are not just metaphors, they are real experiences of leadership and teamwork: it really happened.

As you read on you might just keep in the back of your mind the key leadership questions that we ask any leader to consider:

What does leadership mean to me?

What sort of a leader am I?

What legacy do I want to leave behind as a leader?

In Chapters Two and Three, Alan describes his own immense leadership journeys, in his own words. Chapter Two covers the 'successful failure' as Alan describes it. This was the expedition to the North Pole in 1998 where he and his fellow team member had to be airlifted to safety having faced several life threatening experiences. It is seen as a successful failure because the failure only served to strengthen Alan's resolve to return in 2000 when he succeeded by meticulously implementing lessons learned from the past as well as learning 'in action' throughout the expedition with his fellow adventurers. These are fascinating accounts in their own right, standing alone from consideration in the corporate context. However, in leadership development programmes we always encourage participants to try to compare their own situation with similar situations in a different context. The use of comparison and metaphor is a means of enriching one's own learning. So as you read Alan's account you might consider:

How do the challenges Alan faced compare with mine?

What can I learn from how he has operated as a leader?

What am I going to do differently as a result?

In Chapter Four we have included Alan's post expedition review from the successful 2000 expedition. This covers much of the detail of the expedition and will be of interest to those fascinated by the technicalities of planning, execution and review of the project. This also records for future explorers and adventurers key learning points which it is hoped will provide some tangible benefits.

In Chapter Five, we explore the subject of leadership and the convergence of thinking in terms of the future of leadership and the qualities required as considered from a range of sources including the military and business academics. It can also be seen how Alan has extended his impact to quite different contexts through his organized trips to the North Pole for corporate leaders to international sports teams through his motivational talks.

In Chapter Six, I provide an account of how we approach leadership development using the work based action learning approach. I attempt to debunk some of the myths I feel have emerged in the corporate world of leadership development, about how we should conduct and evaluate the effectiveness of educational programmes. The context here is not the arctic world, but the corporate and business world. However, we hope you will see a number of parallels and by combining the arctic story with the corporate one we have then sought to draw out the key learning points.

A number of perspectives on leadership are provided in Chapter Seven in the form of short sections on leadership and the development of leadership capabilities. We encourage you to access these in an action-based way. You may want to dip in and out, to read relevant sections and then to try things out in practice. After all, leadership is about doing. The aim is to stimulate your thinking and to enable you to take action and to move, perhaps one step at a time, towards becoming the leader you want to be.

So gradually book moves from considering leadership and learning in the context of the polar expeditions to the context of the corporate world. It is not a case of either / or. Leadership is required in both contexts.

2 - The Successful Failure

By Richard Hale & Alan Chambers

Alan Chambers continues a powerful tradition as a British polar adventurer. He describes himself more as an adventurer rather than an explorer, recognizing the pioneering leadership of explorers such as Cook, Ross, Franklin, Scott and Shackleton.

In 1773 James Cook leading a Royal Navy excursion achieved the first crossing of the Antarctic Circle. He thought there was a continent to be discovered but was killed by Hawaiians in 1779 and naval expeditions there halted for forty years.

James Ross was the first to reach the Magnetic North Pole in 1831. He then went south, discovering great ice barriers and volcanoes in the Antarctic and paving the way for Scott, Shackleton and Amdundsen to follow.

The admiralty had long sought after a North-West Passage to the Indies and it was Captain Sir John Franklin who had travelled with Ross in the south, who went north in 1845 and was lost with 129 naval officers. Over thirty expeditions were sent to find Franklin in the seas north of Canada. In 1875 Captain Sir George Nares reached for the North Pole and got to within 400 miles but at the cost of four lives of his crew.

It was with the support of Clement Markham, a Franklin search veteran, navy man and geographer and Honorary Secretary of the Royal Geographic Society, that Scott was selected and mentored to lead major expeditions to the Antarctic. He led the *Discovery* expedition 1901-1904 and then the ill fated *Terra Nova* expedition 1910-1913. Shackleton is often positioned in the history books as a rival of Scott, yet he had learned from his early experiences with Scott and indeed Scott was able to make good use in his *Terra Nova* expedition of the data and discoveries from Shackleton's 1908 *Nimrod* expedition. Yes, clearly there was rivalry but these explorers were born into an era of gentlemanly British competition. Whether they all played strictly by the unwritten rules is another matter, and certainly it would seem that that on occasions one would seek to steal a march on another perhaps by cautious disclosure and selective timing of expedition plans.

Roald Amundsen, the Norwegian who ultimately was successful in beating Scott to the South Pole, clearly did not play by the rules of the British public school or Royal Navy. As the great British explorer Sir Ranulph Fiennes points out in his excellent biography of Scott, *Captain Scott*, Amundsen was not too selective in terms of whom he deceived, be it his sponsors, government or his own crew, let alone perceived competitor explorers. He was not out to conduct scientific research, which was a major part of Scott's mission, he was hell-bent on beating the British to the South Pole.

These expeditions often entailed spending years at a time away from home and loved ones, and step by painful step discovering new territories, christening the land and the ice territories they found with the names of their monarchs, or friends and relations. They achieved this whilst seeking to achieve new routes and often whilst conducting serious scientific research. They experimented with new technologies, clothing and equipment. At the same time they were working out from their own experience and by sharing experiences amongst each other, how best to navigate different territory, deciding whether, where and when to use dogs, ponies, manhaul or mechanized transport. There were no known answers to many of these problems and frequently the excursions from base camps led to the most terrible journeys and experiences. Often they made the ultimate sacrifice, as in the case of Scott and many of his team.

Alan Chambers' heroes are these early explorers and he recognizes the severe physical and mental challenges they faced with unproven equipment and without the technologies we have today. Of modern day explorers he has immense respect for Sir Ranulph Fiennes and others referred to in the acknowledgements section of this book. No doubt Alan as with these historic explorers of their day, is subject to what the Norwegians call *polarhüller*, the draw of the extremes of polar world. He has plans for further polar expeditions to both poles and a vision for supporting Inuit communities. In between expeditions he takes business leaders to the North Pole for trips where they all take part in leading the group and seeking to achieve their diverse personal goals. He also shares with the historic explorers an interest in innovation, constantly seeking to refine his practice and improve performance, whether through diet, clothing or transportation. In this sense Alan follows a great tradition of polar explorers and adventurers; he is, like they were, an action learner. He learns from his experience and from his research. He learns from others from the past and present and is open to learning from those he walks with, many who have significantly less polar experience than him.

Here, Alan describes who he is and what he has achieved. He provides a brief introduction to his life in the military and then discusses his life as an adventurer and explorer. He tells the story of the first attempt to reach the North Pole unsupported in 1998. In one sense it is a story of failure, but it might be considered failure that that only served to increase his inner drive ultimately to succeed.

In 1984 at the age of 16 I joined the Royal Marine Commandos in England and spent the next 15 years travelling the world on and off operations. The training is the hardest military basic training in the world. It lasts a testing 30 weeks. Experiencing life and cultures across the globe over those 15 years helped form me as a person. Being in tight situations and having not only to lead men but to think and react on my feet, with the weight of others lives in my hands, taught me lessons and skills I soon harnessed.

There was more to reality, than the rough and tumble of commando life and wherever I saw an opportunity to break away from the norm I did. Jumping ship from Gibraltar after operations in the Middle East, two of us cycled back to England, a mere seventeen hundred miles, roughing it each night and pedalling over one hundred miles a day. From the roads of Spain and France I decided to join a team to become the first people to ski across Iceland in the world.

The trip was to last 47 days, dragging 240 pound sledges across 500 miles of semi-frozen ice-covered volcanic wasteland. It had never been successfully traversed in six previous attempts. A great deal was learned, regarding teamwork and hidden agendas. The late Princess Diana graciously gave her time and support. We had an audience with her at Kensington Palace for promotional photographs and she supported the trip in its entirety. The added bonus of skiing across Iceland was that we managed to raise £50,000 for spinal research and promote the awareness of people who could not walk. I personally learned a great deal about evaluating people and finding their concealed or secret aspirations. What really drove people to go the extra mile and in some cases not. It was a great stepping stone towards what would become a journey into the history books.

Two years later I spent three months living with the Inuit Eskimos during their dark winter, assessing all kinds of equipment and making my own evaluations. I was ticking off the mental hang-ups in my mind, relying only on myself as the judge and jury in considering whether it was achievable and I was up to it. Not only did we mentally train but also physically we walked from the graves of the ill-fated Franklin expedition of 1845. These guys were a true inspiration to me on the coldest days of my life, a killing minus seventy-two °C. Certain death without extraordinary motivation.

Success or Failure? The 1998 Expedition to the North Pole.

I could not believe what he had just done! I really couldn't accept he would do something so bloody selfish. What was going through his mind? Why would he decide to call an irreversible halt to this expedition without really asking or communicating with me?

My mind found this hard to compute after all we have been through just to get to the start point. I had to control my hellish anger at that moment because we were still over 800 miles away from any form of civilization, and we still needed each other's physical, if not mental support, before we can escape this devil's labyrinth of ice.

After three years intense planning and research to determine what could be eight weeks trudging through hell and back to the North Pole to achieve ultimate success, we are now in an emergency situation where the odds are against us for survival.

Between 1995 and early March 1998 our two-man team had persuaded the gods that we could make a serious attempt to walk to the Geographic North Pole from Canada unsupported, and claim to be the first British team to do so. We thought we had covered every angle of planning and after knowing each other for some ten years the question about compatibility and cohesion was foolishly dismissed. Why? Because we were to set off on what I believed was a venture forged by joint beliefs, aims, convictions and finally goals. How wrong could I be?

I emerged from our temporary home, a little dome tent, to a sight that was beyond belief. The other half of our two-man team is standing quite happily in front of what can only be described as a raging inferno. The glow of the flames lit the darkness of the Arctic night, and the heat from the belly of the fire is alien to its surroundings. What had he done? And why?

Since we set off from Ward Hunt Island 13 days ago on this joint dream, we had encountered quite a few alarming equipment problems, especially at such an early stage of the expedition. The most horrifying had been the loss of fuel within the sledges, which had not only contaminated the food supplies, but also forced us to contingency plan from almost the outset of our journey.

The fuel was swilling around inside our sledges, covering all that it came in contact with. Not only was our food reeking with fuel, but our sleeping bags were soaking with white gas and the fumes would linger during the night, giving the tired and weary adventurer one hell of a headache.

With all the will and desire in the world and with all the inner passion and drive to succeed, it is food that carries us forward. Food that fuels our success, food that in turn keeps us from going mad. After ten hours of hauling a 200 pound sledge over ice boulders, you have only two things to look forward to: food and sleep.

With the abundance of our food supply contaminated, and already divided in our true and inner aims, the expedition was always going to be twice as tough. Then a second fuel spillage meant we had to really contemplate our position. What with our entire power supply of lithium batteries also having failed, we needed to seriously reconsider our next move. Our initial conversation contemplating failure was not a great success for many reasons, and I had soon buried my head in my diary to recalculate what serviceable food and fuel we had left and how we could reconfigure the master plan so we could keep walking. Admittedly it would have had to be on a supported basis after a re-supply, but we could still have re-planned and still carried on. Still have kept walking.

I had already lost faith in the overall planning, the big scheme of things, a few months before departing England. So to reassess and choose whether to push on was something I needed to come to terms with in my own way, in my own mind, trusting only myself and relying on my own sanity as my sole advocate.

Knowing myself, once I have all the boxes ticked off in my mind the next move is then taken with a whole heart, unwavering confidence and 150 percent effort and trust.

The raging fire was now the glow of a shattered dream, the embodiment of failure. I approached the pit to see, in horror, all our food supplies and all the remaining fuel, stockpiled and in flames. The only part of this trip that now has any chance of making it to the North Pole is a piece of floating ash being carried north by the arctic breeze.

You selfish bastard! The mirror between us is now shattered and once it is broken, well, you know the rest.

We had enough food and fuel to last us three days. It had just taken us two weeks to reach the point where we stood and camped.

Three days' food? Let's hope the rescue plane can land and extract a team that now has a divide the width of the Red Sea.

A divide that can never be bridged again.

I feel I have been stripped of the facility to even share my thinking and planning processes. I can't even bring myself to voice an opinion on a contingency plan to try and regain some success. I have been rudely and violently awakened from a dream, a dream that has been selfishly turned into a nightmare with the strike of a single match. Thanks!

There is a fine line between determination and stubbornness. Knowing myself, I sit smack bang on the seat in the middle. I have no choice: no options, no contingency, and now no faith in the nucleus of people back home called a team. I know my stubbornness will get me back to base camp and in turn back to normal work, but I also know deep down my determination must turn this adversity around, and pull out every drop of positive feedback from this awful plight.

This will fuel, with focused rage what will be my next move…another attempt to the North Pole but with a determined, passionate and befitting team.

We aren't safe from danger by a long way. With only survival amounts of food between us and a rapidly diminishing fuel supply we are now destined to a silent time waiting for the pick-up by the search and rescue plane. The base camp know exactly where we are by satellite positioning and they know we are at least 48 hours' away from any form of pick-up.

The weather has now taken a turn for the worse and we are struggling to erect the tent in the brim of a storm.

Once the decision, as selfish as it is, has been taken to abort the walk, your body immediately starts to feel the cold, pains and aches it would normally reject because of the inner drive and centred passion that would push it through these mental and physical barriers. Now completely dejected and depressed with the thought of an early return, any form of exertion is ten times as difficult.

We know the plane will need a long relatively flat ice runway to land on. The next ten hours or so are spent with our two tiny shovels out on a smooth pan of ice trying to squash and break down any larger lumps of sastrugi. This is fine. I can be four to five hundred metres away from the tent and in a world of thoughts all to myself.

Once spare clothing marks the runway, made up mainly of upturned salopettes, we are just about done. This will be the last few hours on the pack ice waiting in silence for the sound of the twin otter engine.

The atmosphere between us is horrible. Once I get pissed off I know I go very quiet and withdraw to reflect on exactly what is going on, and how this situation has occurred. The pack ice is a quiet place, an unearthly serene domain with no noise to spoil such a tranquil expanse of frozen tundra.

We don't have to wait too long before we hear the gentle purr of the aeroplane quickly turn into a welcoming roar overhead.

Once we make voice communication with the two pilots it should be just a matter of moments until we are safely extracted and on our return journey back to base camp and civilization. A routine flight for the crew. Every year they fly out to different degrees of latitude to rescue the floundered adventurer who is in jeopardy.

The voice of the pilot is like a breath of fresh air in our tent. There is such an atmosphere between us; as sullen as if a death had occurred. We are both now out of the tent, injected with life again, thinking we are out of this dreadful predicament. The pilots, who are probably the best in the world, will now try for hours to land on the rough sea ice. Pass after pass, knocking the crowns of frozen mounds of ice trying to smooth out the landing strip.

In the back of my mind after the first three passes the alarm bells are ringing. How many passes can he perform and still have enough fuel to get him and the co-pilot home safely?

At the end of the day the pilot's lives would take precedence over any emergency situation. When all your hopes are on that little plane to extract you, the reality of this fact seems, very frustrating. But the pilots did not ask us to come into their country and try to walk unsupported to the Pole, so we had but two people to blame…ourselves.

The dreaded words arrive, crackling over the radio, words I will never forget. To fail a task, to have to live and breathe an ocean of excuses to the sponsors and friends was daunting enough. I am a firm believer that once the mind weakens, the body will crumble. We have come to terms with the fact that in a short temporary way that this was the end. Now all we need to do is get on the plane and face the flak. If only it was that easy!

Those frightful words boomed from the radio set.

'I am so sorry guys we cannot land, I say again we cannot land…'

I never thought my heart could sink any further, to prolong this agony was the equivalent to torture.

The next voice over the radio is the co-pilot:

'Polar North, Polar North, we do not have enough fuel left to land in an alternative landing site. You must return to Ward Hunt Island where we will pick you up in 48 hours. There is a strong weather front approaching and if you do not make it to Ward Hunt Island in time it could be up to two weeks until our next fly over!'

When you think that you have failed not only yourself but also everybody involved in the venture, and it seems the whole world knows you have not achieved your goal and aspiration, your mind plays tricks on you. You have the arctic angel on one shoulder and the polar devil on the opposite side. Both telling you what is right and what you should do. Both so-called advocates attempting to lure you into being somebody else.

The human mind finds that it wants to always take the easy option. As soon as your mind agrees to this your body spirals at a rapid rate into a huge sense of false security. It creates a comfort zone that can get you through the immediate dilemma, yet no further.

To be able to recognize and favour the harder decision and option, which you know will both physically and mentally be many times harder, is a skill and gift you only know you possess once you hold your life and other team members' lives in your hand.

It is not normal to always pick out the arduous way and constantly choose to put oneself through turmoil and mental anguish, but the rewards after deciding on the onerous path are massive.

So what makes a person step out of themselves to become somebody they have yet never been? The inner gift of survival, a survival to want to live and love your life. That is the element that transforms a situation of possible death into a situation of possible further life and enjoyment.

As a leader, you must take this gift to a much higher level. Each individual in your team is worth as much, if not more than you are yourself. I say gift because there are relatively few people who naturally can turn adversity and disaster into gratification and success.

We now face the daunting task of struggling to Ward Hunt Island, our original start point. In the short time we have spent on the ice a lot has happened, and more importantly, a lot has deteriorated. The trek back to where we started from, over all that unforgiving ice and fearsome open water that half killed us, is going to be daunting to say the least.

Most of the decisions have already been made for us because of our lack of food, however we still have some life saving decisions to make as a team. Our best move now is to abandon the majority of the equipment and make the sledges lighter and more manageable. Our hearts and souls are not really in the trip any more and it is more a case of safety and the chance of survival, than genuine teamwork and collaboration.

It has taken us thirteen days to reach this point and we had only 48 hours to return over some of the most inhospitable terrain in the world.

We have to make the deadline and we have to do it by pure determination and guts. After a hot meal and a pint of hot drink we set off into the teeth of a blizzard; just what we don't need. The storm is blowing fresh snow in all directions and the navigation soon becomes quite difficult. Our mental strength has been drained due to the awful circumstances of our return, which in turn is making the progress very slow.

Up until the day of disaster we were walking about eight hours a day, maximum. I know this speed will not get us to the start point and the rendezvous with our freedom bird out of the Arctic Ocean. We have only 48 hours. So we pick up the pace, our minds driving each one of our steps, faster than our bodies are willing to go but not as fast as we know we need to go now that survival is our primary objective.

The first day is horrific, the feeling of failure and dejection overpowering the instinct of wanting to survive. We manage to push on as a team of two for 14 hours, through the worst weather I have ever experienced.

We are chilled to the bone and completely exhausted. When you walk in to the belly of a blizzard your face freezes to a waxy solid state. You soon forget how cold your bones and digits are really feeling. The sensation of numbness is quickly forgotten because the emotion of complete emptiness takes over.

Every inch of flesh has to be covered in these extreme temperatures. It is early fall and with the wind chill, the temperature is now an unfathomable -65°C. The molecules of fluid within the skin cells will freeze in seconds. If you turn into the wind, the film of fluid that covers your eye will freeze and make shutting the eye or blinking extremely painful.

Time after time both sets of eyelashes are freezing together, and when you are wearing five pairs of mittens the delicate task of releasing the eyelids becomes blundered which in turn masks your vision momentarily. The moment of vision or blindness could be that moment when you need your best judgement. Even the simplest task is so laboriously painful.

I thought the night time would never come. It descends all right and I keep on walking through the blizzard and south towards Ward Hunt Island. *'We will make it no matter what'* I keep saying this to myself over and over again.

We finally call a stop to the first leg of the epic struggle home and erected the tent in the storm and made sure we anchored all sides of the tent down with everything we had. We still needed this teamwork. Ice boulder after ice boulder was wedged against the tent sides, in the hope it would not lift off during the strong winds. The situation could only have got worse if we had lost our tent. It was our only protection from the increasing bad weather that was tearing us apart.

That night we did not have to go through the time-consuming process of melting enough ice to fill all eight flasks like normal, so the cooking time was relatively short. This suited me fine; I was completely exhausted and just wanted this chapter of the journey over.

We arose the next morning after only a few hours sleep. The storm had kept us both awake even though we were exhausted. The noises of the wind firing ice particles against the sides of the tent like speeding bullets, was ear piercing. The howling wind seemed to be talking to us within the tent, telling me *'You will have to dig deeper than you have ever dug before to get yourself out of this momentous plight.'*

Nature was testing my mind by delivering us doses of hell, one after another after another. At that moment I did not fully appreciate what a forbidding but important lesson I was being taught.

If you have a poor night's sleep in the arctic, the next day manhauling is usually twice as strenuous; firstly, because of the tired muscles, and secondly, because you waste mental energy pondering why you were not sleeping. We had only 24 hours before the plane was due to land. 24 hours left of the weather window that could extract us from this netherworld. Once the tent was packed away, we set off in the typical fashion of one person leading, the other following.

Like two zombies, the walking dead, we had to trudge on south, hoping the blizzard will ease and relax, and the walk would become easier. We managed to push on through biting winds and relentless cold. Our bodies were just going through the motions – one foot after another, mindlessly creeping forward.

We had to negotiate around open stretches of water that have now formed, which meant that the weary mind had to channel all its ability to think laterally and positively. Once we were safe from a possible swim, the mind then settled back into zombie mode.

Every step was demoralizing, knowing we had once covered this ground before only a few days ago. We were now within spitting distance of shelter.

We walked off the edge of the pack ice and moved on to the ice shelf. This shelf would lead us to the sanctuary of wooden huts that were built many years before by some great adventurers. The very idea of being able to detach from this storm was enough to keep walking.

Once we are safe in the huts all we have to do is await the search and rescue plane. It will also give us time to contemplate the future. Two separate futures at that. In the distance through all the spindrift we saw the shape of big half dome wooden huts and out-buildings. We were close. Ward Hunt Island, our start point, a tethered Canadian flag flapping in the wind with the passion of a fighting gladiator. I never thought it possible but I was extremely pleased to see these huts. However, they are a materialistic statement of failure, because I never expected to be back at the start; but I was past that feeling now, and looking for out.

Once you can see your immediate goal, your last few steps seem to be under a burden of pressure, a hardship that feels like the weight of the world is being slowly but surely pressed down onto your shoulders. The final physical effort must now be fuelled by the inner drive we must have held at sometime to want to attempt the seemingly impossible. Those minute wooden huts soon grow in size and meaning.

The closer we walked to them the closer I was to being able to express a huge sigh of relief. The final hurdle was no picnic and the last few steps were just as arduous as the first few. We had made it against the odds; we had managed to reach a more sensible state of safety. Fatigued and drained of all physical and mental strength, we got into the shelters to await the blessed pickup plane.

We'd battled against human endurance and everything nature could deal us, compounded with the ever-niggling thought of 'why are we walking backwards?'. Failure. We had beaten the odds, and now would be able to relax. Or would we?

The overpowering feeling of exhaustion soon was extinguished from our minds. To our horror, what should have taken a few moments to get into the shelter and light our stoves and try to make use of the cover, turned into yet another hourly task of perseverance. There was what seemed to be a snowdrift banked against the entrance, some five feet high and five feet thick.

The wind driven snow had compacted into a solid barrier of ice. I shook my head in disbelief; this could not get any worse. Please somebody explain what had we done do deserve this further suffering?

With the storm now dying down and visibility returning to a stable few metres, we scouted around searching for any larger shovels to make the task of entering the shelter quicker and not so tiring. Nothing could be found so we had to remove this ton of packed snow by hand using the small shovels from our sledges. Finally, after pooling all our last strength, we managed to dig our way into the shelter. We had removed enough snow and ice from the entrance, so we could prise open the door and squeeze in. Thank God!

It was not long before we were settled in the hut, trying to re-warm our frozen and weary bodies using our stoves. We searched around the hut looking for tales of past explorers and adventures.

We read diaries from the people who have built the huts to inject new thoughts into our minds. This would hide the fact that we were on our way home after failure. The hut was indescribably cold; it seemed colder than the hellish terrain we had just spent the last two weeks living in. It was a small price to pay while we waited to be picked up, a small price to pay after what we had just experienced both physically and mentally.

The atmosphere in the hut replicates the one in the tent after the inferno. One of stubbornness and conflicting thoughts. By now I don't care as such. The altercation that happened on the ice has happened and now we have safely returned to our start point. The next physical step for us is to fly back to base camp in Resolute Bay and await details of the return journey home to the UK. For me it is now a time to contemplate my next move.

It was not long before I heard the gentle, distant purr of the Twin Otter rescue plane in the air above the roof of this cold sanctuary, only a few miles to our south. This was the noise of joy. My expedition to the Geographic North Pole finished here with this divorce of friendship and trust.

I made a silent promise to return to this forbidden place, a promise to try and turn the failure and adversity around to work in my favour, a promise to make the impossible possible.

To be inspired by failure and defeat takes special qualities. Qualities of strong character and judgement. Self-motivation was driving me to want to return, to deposit myself back in hell...

On our return we were invited to Buckingham Palace in London for an evening meant for young achievers. In my mind we did not fit into that category or deserve any formal recognition. The word 'failure' has a demoralizing meaning to most people. The failure in 1998 wasn't entirely in that context. Only one in 150 million people attempt the walk we tried, so at least we had tried.

A telegram was received from Buckingham Palace:

BUCKINGHAM PALACE

MESSAGE FROM THE CAPTAIN GENERAL ROYAL MARINES

TO :   CORPORAL ALAN CHAMBERS

     I AM SORRY TO HEAR THAT YOU HAVE HAD TO ABANDON
THE NORTH POLE PROJECT. IT IS ALWAYS A NASTY DECISION TO
GIVE UP, BUT DISCRETION IS BETTER THAN DISASTER.

PHILIP

FRIDAY, 3RD APRIL, 1998

3 - Ultimate Success

By Alan Chambers

In 2000 Alan launched what was to be the successful expedition to reach the North Pole unsupported, travelling by the most difficult route from Canada. He turned the adversity of 1998 ultimately into a success that would see him achieve a place in the history of exploration. This expedition would test him further, physically and mentally, at a personal level and as a leader.

After the successful failure in 1998, I did not see the next attempt as a challenge but as an opportunity. An opportunity to put the records straight, but more importantly, to prove what high performance and well structured teamwork could achieve when combined with strong true leadership. Leadership that would set a precedent, hopefully for future adventurers and businesses world-wide, and show the world what could be achieved both physically and mentally against all odds. We had only a one percent chance of success as judged by the critics. They say a man who lives out his dreams is a scary man. I scared myself; however, it was my choice. Life holds a certain risk; the more alive you are, the more the risk. It seemed natural to me to re-plan meticulously for the millennium walk. I spent the next two years searching for approval to go. I begged, stole and borrowed equipment and had the daunting task of procuring all the capital finance within three weeks. I researched into the last 25 years of failed attempts for the reason why they failed. I then calculated or programmed a solution to their failures, into my master plan.

My biggest venture was to recruit volunteers and convey my inner passion into their souls. I had a dream and wanted to live it out. I needed to build a team from strangers, from scratch, with the only common motivation of wanting to walk north. Five training evolutions later and after 500 hours in the gym or dragging truck tyres, and eventually being fully funded and sponsored, we were on our way. To get to the start point was my hardest task. Without being conceited, once I was there on my own with my men, in my mind, soul and heart we could not fail.

After forwarding the freight to Canada from the UK over the Christmas period, we were all set to go. We left our loved ones at home on a cold damp February day arriving at our base camp location 48 hours later. It was a biting -50°C as we stepped off the plane, a great reality check for us all. I conducted emergency procedures out on the ice straight away, trying to cover every eventuality that might arise. One procedure would later save a team member's life on two separate occasions. He can carry on living and enjoying life because of a team structured around trust and integrity. It was the final testing ground before I took my hopes and dreams to play the devil at arctic roulette. Time to tie all the loose ends into a rope that would be strong enough to hold the team through many life and death situations. A rope that soon became a lifeline. After only seven days at base camp , we were chomping at the bit and ready for what was to be one of the worst journeys in the world.

After a seven hour flight, the Twin Otter aircraft dropped us at our start point: Ward Hunt Island. For me it brought back memories of 1998 and the near-death experience trying to find these shelters in the blizzard. For the rest of the team it was a triumph in its own right just to reach the start point. Another mental hurdle for me was to reach further north than I did previously. It was time to turn that spell of adversity into positive leg muscle and ski action. The immediate time was spent ironing out all the niggling problems, and I evaluated the team under immense mental pressure and extraordinary physical strain. Each person was pulling a sledge laden with stores to last eight weeks; the weight was 250 pounds, the equivalent to a baby elephant. Each person was responsible for getting that weight across the polar desert until we called a halt for the day. However, on many occasions we all had to harness to one sledge and drag one at a time then return for the others one by one. I had decided to walk the hardest way possible to the North Pole by going against the drift, so each night we would drift backwards, pushed rearwards by the arctic currents. And to go unsupported was the most demanding challenge in the world. People call it the horizontal Everest, and more men have stood on the moon than have walked to the North Pole. I led from the front for the first three days and each minute looked back to see my men struggling with the sledge and equally struggling with their own minds, asking themselves why they were there and what the hell did they volunteer for? It was this cancerous mind game I needed to find a cure for immediately, or the team would crumble. Had my preparations been thorough? Had I installed true passion into my men? A passion that could save their lives when confronted with the arctic reaper.

Exhaustive frustration can be the only way to describe trying to conquer this abyss of this relentless, unforgiving desert of ice. Each day we arose to a frozen interior of the tent. The frost dangled, awaiting the slightest movement or exhalation before it fell confidently onto your face. Each morning was torture, just trying to motivate oneself enough to get out of the damp sleeping bag and face the world at -45°C. The human adventurer, who is proving to himself that he can overcome all, poisons the eerie silence of this arctic wasteland by uncontrollably shivering just to keep his vital organs working. We struggled each day, only making a few metres progress in half a day's haul. We would walk across open expanses of level ice that acted as honey to a bee, straight into the middle of huge boulder fields. Each field would be up to five miles square if not more, and each boulder could stand as tall as 50 feet. It was like walking in a land of giants. There was no easy way out; all we could do was select the premium route through this demoralizing maze of glacial rubble. People were now starting to let their minds run their bodies, that in turn would start to corrupt that passion I had instilled. From this early point I confronted their true aspirations and was rewarded with varying degrees of returned honesty.

I knew from past experience that to walk 500 miles in these conditions would always seem impossible. For this reason alone I broke the expedition down into seven stages. Seven achievable goals. Seven separate aims. As meticulous as I was, I had worked out how much fuel, food and energy we would need per stage. This was my master plan. The 'keep walking' scheme. We managed to hit stage one four days early. This was great for team spirit and mental focus. We did the same for stage two and evened out on stage three. It was working: 'plan for the worst and hope for the best.' My strategy was working. The team was building in confidence and faith because we had actually achieved positive results and could see that we could control the pace and still achieve our goals. Mentally the plan was worth its weight in gold. Everything was running smoothly, until the first in a catalogue of horrific near-death incidents occurred.

Charlie tumbled from a huge ice boulder, seriously damaging the tissues and muscles in his back. Then if that was not enough, he fell through a weak part of the frozen ocean and started to panic. Fortunately leadership instinct took over and the team's emergency procedure kicked into place and we managed to drag him to safety and start to re-warm his chilled and wet body. Eventually we were able to save him. The next morning to show he had kept his nerve Charlie led the first leg and after only one hour of walking he crashed through the ice again, immediately up to his neck in polar water. The temperature was -35°C. I managed to dash forward, forgetting I had a 200 pound sledge tied to my waist and just grabbed him before his head went under. If we had lost sight of him under the ice we may have never seen him again. It was this tight and trusting teamwork that had saved his life. I felt responsible, but greatly relieved personally for him and myself. Relieved that I had had the foresight to rehearse this procedure just in case. How delighted I was. However, logistically this caused detrimental changes to the 'keep walking' plan. I had to think laterally and adapt our strategy. This would be key to the development of mental strength later needed and eventually the accomplishment.

We stood waiting for all Charlie's clothing to become absolutely bone dry. I could not expect any member of the team to start walking in damp clothing, as it would freeze instantly causing frostbite. Whilst we were waiting I had revamped the plan and made the necessary changes which were to help us triumph. After Charlie's second fall he naturally lost all confidence in leading his leg and being out in front. From that moment I knew this dwindling confidence could soon stretch in to the rest of the team, so I took action. I crossed every stretch of refrozen open water first. Any frozen lead no matter how small or large I unharnessed and free skied across, until I found a suitable route or until I decided the ice was not stable and would endanger life. Each step I held my breath, the only noise breaking the arctic silence the thumping of my distressed heartbeat. Once across I would then ski back, hook up my sledge and cross again with the added weight. Once safely across I would un-harness, ski out to the middle again and guide each team member across one at a time until all my ducklings were safe on the other side. Some days I would repeat this procedure twenty to thirty times. Mentally it was very demanding and draining for me, but how could I expect them to attempt such risk without me making sure it was possible to even try. To be a leader means exactly that. It was my choice, therefore my responsibility, no one else's. One evening after a long slog, Paul removed his set of mittens in the tent. He was experiencing feeling a burning sensation all over his thumb. Straight away it was glaringly obvious he was suffering from extreme, hellish frostbite and needed immediate medical attention. His finger had turned coal black and had doubled in size, forming huge blisters. As a team we needed to make a decision and as a leader I had to be 100 percent correct with my final choice of action. I felt sympathetic and sorry for Paul as he had accomplished the hardest physical stage of the expedition in the coldest temperatures, over the most grueling ground. How this had happened is still beyond any explanation and I find it hard to comprehend that it did happen unnoticed. However, it had and I needed to take responsibility. After two days of what must have been a painful thought process for Paul, he selflessly decided to leave the trip for the good of the expedition. A courageous and brave decision.

Full-hearted, I accepted what was the best option and started to initiate an emergency evacuation for a very downhearted and dejected team member. Whilst waiting for the rescue plane Jason was doubled in agony with acute kidney and liver failure. He decided to leave too. This was a calculated and sincere decision and made my life easier. If he had not chosen to vacate I would have had to insist he left as we only had enough money in the kitty for one pick-up. So in a matter of three days the team was now a duo. Could I re-plan and contingency plan for the rest of the walk with me and the least experienced member of the team? Did I have enough self-belief and understanding of our strengths and weaknesses to make that call correctly? How would we cope with only two sets of hands instead of four? Had I bitten off more than I can chew? If two had deteriorated would we be next? Was I taking too much risk? A million and one questions were spontaneously exploding in and out of my mind while we were waiting for the rescue plane. Did I have the courage to lead on? I was accountable to all, including our next of kin. It was an emotional tearful departure for those two brave men.

We still had over 300 miles to negotiate as the polar pair, and with the past setbacks we were now behind time. We needed to jettison some of our equipment to give ourselves any hope of making up the time and distance lost waiting for the rescue plane. Whilst we had been static awaiting the Twin Otter plane, we had drifted 360 nautical miles east towards Greenland and, more devastatingly, four miles south. So once again, we had to salvage lost ground. However, we kept one another going and focused, by our relentless sense of humour and leg pulling and our common ability to laugh at each other in times of crisis and total exhaustion. We were starting to form a bond that would last forever. Charlie became a rock upon the polar icecap; an honest, reliable, trustworthy tower of character. I owe him a great deal. We started to cement then what has turned into a great friendship. However strongly we performed as a team, though, this never alleviated the fact that we still had to personally drive one foot in front of the other and haul what was still a painstakingly heavy load over every inch of frozen wasteland. The temperature was now a mild -30°C. The toil of dragging a baby elephant across the top of the world had taken its toll. We had deteriorated in muscle and strength. It was Catch 22, mind over matter and the will to survive to the end. The weather and ice conditions were rapidly deteriorating and we had trouble negotiating the semi-frozen pans of open water. The unforgiving razor sharp ice had perforated our sledges that were designed to float as rafts, so we could not paddle across any more open water. This meant each time we had to find a way or make one, using huge ice boulders as temporary bridges. The downside was it would take a great amount of time, energy and hardship to constantly build bridge after bridge. A lot of time was squandered by having to detour around vast open expanses of water. This in turn meant we were consuming too many days' food because of the extra mileage. Once again we needed to re-think the plan through. I made a decision to cut the food into quarter bags and ration us. The downside was our body weight and strength deteriorated rapidly, bringing with it a mentally fatigued state which also a triggered us to take more risks. I fell through the ice twice and Charlie yet again. Why were we punishing ourselves to such an inhuman level? Previously we had survived two possible fatal tent fires by our swift reactions - could we do it again in such an overworked state of mental anguish?

I had a cold nervous feeling rushing over my body, a confused state of unnerving panic. I knew something was wrong but I was still half asleep in the early hours of this chilling arctic dawning. My subconscious was registering danger, but I could not quite put my finger on it.

It was not polar bears, because the noise outside was far too great. In my experience with direct contact of these immense, majestically intelligent killers, I have found them as nervous as the human. So it wasn't polar bears and we were too far north for wolves.

My thoughts were trying to interpret the noise, while scrambling for the shotgun, just in case I was wrong about the bears. My mind was alert but wearied and was working at a sluggish frozen speed, trying to compute all the different sensations from all the available senses. Then I knew, without leaving the security of the tent, what was happening. Shit!

I quickly clothed myself, making sure I had enough layers on just to view the danger and stay out long enough to formulate a decision, the best one I could, at haste. My mind was working overtime; like someone had directly injected caffeine into me. Charlie was now waking from his Scottish dreams of bagpipes, haggis and porridge, wondering what was going on and why I was opening the tent door at this ungodly hour. What he wasn't aware of was all those initial thoughts of fear and uneasiness that had travelled in and out of my mind making my heart race and toes curl with anxiety.

In a way I am pleased only I had to deal with those panicked moments. It is better only one of us use our precious mental energy, so that the other team member has no need to worry himself over problems. He might have to make a more complex and spontaneous life-saving decision immediately after I left the tent, so he had to be fully charged.

My final assumption before leaving the tent was positively confirmed as I slowly stretched my head and neck out into the biting cold. Even though I was staring at a potentially deadly situation, my first reaction was to laugh, and laugh I did.

There had been many, many times on the trip when I thought the entire world was against us and we were fated never to achieve our destiny. I still believed in myself as an individual whose passion was the driving force of this team, and I maintained that our strategy was flexible enough to take on all comers. You can plan for the worst and hope for the best. I tried to plan for every possible scenario so I had an antidote to every problem that potentially could derail the team from our original plans.

40

So when we were facing immediate disaster it was not a shock or surprise. This enabled me to think on my feet, but more importantly, think laterally in a rational, prepared manner under seemingly great stress. This meant I could bounce the team back with a more resilient outlook for the next difficulty. We were in no place to learn by failure, which is a natural part of the success process, but we had to learn by giving ourselves options. Options to progress forward and achieve our set aims.

I hadn't planned for this though. I think that was the reason why I was laughing. What is the point in wailing, getting frustrated or enraged. For the first time on the trip our destiny laid precariously in the hands of another…the hands of Mother Nature. We had to play her game at the moment, but in my mind I knew we could outsmart her and catch her off guard. We would not be beaten yet. Each time Charlie and I overcame adversity he shouted to the sky, 'you will have to do better than that!' and on one occasion she nearly had.

The ocean had been grinding and groaning mid-morning one sunny day and we noticed that there was a lot of shifting ice all around us, and devastatingly to us, directly on our intended path. We managed to increase our speed to try and obtain some distance away from the unstable platform we were on and tried to get to a high ice boulder to pick an alternative route, when we had the fright of our lives.

A crack had appeared right in front of our eyes; splitting and breaching the frozen ocean like a hot knife would cut through a lump of butter. We had quickly dragged our sledges over the increasingly widening gap just in time. As we had turned around to admire our victory, the ocean erupted and the force of the tides closed the gap in seconds, crushing all that was in its way. Soon it had formed a divide of broken ice some ten metres high, as far as the eye could see to the east and west.

This all happened in the space of a few minutes. We had stood there happy and smug, delighted that we had crossed the gap before it formed into this huge barrier of ice. All cocky we had sat on our sledges and laughed with a pride of accomplishment, and once again Charlie had shouted, 'you will have to do better than that.'

As soon as he said 'that' there had been an almighty thunderous boom, and the frozen ocean directly beneath our feet had started to force open, revealing the deadly darkness of the ten thousand feet deep watery grave. The cockiness subsided in a nanosecond and we had sped across the ice with all our might until we were away from the rift and the open water. Our hearts were racing and we were soon doubled over gasping for breath; which, when you are inhaling ice cold air that burns your lungs on entry, is not a comfortable position to be in.

It was Mother Nature giving us a reminder that she held the deck and not to become too complacent. I had to draw on every lesson that we had learned on our journey. I drew on every drop of positive wisdom and knowledge I could and I recalled that someone once told me 'only a fool makes the same mistake twice.' How true.

By now Charlie had managed to put his boots on the correct feet and stumbled out of the tent to see what all the commotion was about; he too laughed. I believe the ability to laugh in dangerous, formidable situations is a gift. A quality that allows your mind time to comprehend what you are facing, and ultimately what you will have to deal with in the imminent future. It gives you that extra split second, which stops you from reacting irrationally or in the completely wrong manner. In this climate reacting wrongly could quite easily cause the loss of a team member's life. This would be the ultimate disaster and no personal journey in the world is worth the life of any team member.

Our joint laughter grew and grew until we realized that we were laughing instead of trying to work out what the hell to do. The noise and commotion I heard during the night came from us. It came from the block of ice we had camped upon for the night's recuperation. It came from our section of immediate turf, because we were now detached from the rest of the Arctic Ocean and we were uncontrollably drifting across the ocean towards Greenland.

Each night we tried to find the most stable area of ice that would be firmly secured on at least three sides. There was no full moon looming or just past, so the ocean should have been relatively stable. The previous night we had chosen an area no different in appearance or ice thickness than on any other occasion. So why were we now buoyant, bobbing along at speed on an ice floe no larger that the size of a football pitch?

We both had a good scout around just to weigh up the problem. We conducted a 360° sweep of the area and met back at the tent to compare our findings and create some form of contingency plan. Still both smiling we knew we were not in any immediate danger and discussed our predicament over a hot chocolate drink laced with whisky.

By now I had grown to trust and respect Charlie's judgment on every aspect of arctic travel and would stand by his decision as strongly as he stood by mine. So I knew when he said to me that we are all right for a while he wasn't worried or overly concerned. This meant to me that I shouldn't worry either. We then tried to finish the night's sleep off. Sleep was so important at this stage because our bodies were so weak. We lost a lot of energy each night trying to get to sleep in these awful conditions.

For me the few hours in the sleeping bags were unbearable. My mind was set alight wondering what our options would be; I did not fancy the swim to freedom. More like a swim to sure death. For the first time I was cornered. Mother Nature was not only teaching us a lesson but also was now dictating our course of action and destiny. I wondered sometimes if any being was looking at us from above.

I even thought if Charlie was not so cheeky each time we managed to beat the system, we wouldn't be in this predicament, but that was a ridiculous and selfish thought. What had happened had happened and it was up to me to work this one through. I was confident that we would survive and not only that but we would be able to push on forward and strive north with added confidence and courage.

I had had enough of tossing and turning in my very thin sleeping bag and wanted to get up and assess the situation outside. I convinced myself to put it off and put it off many times because I did not want to deprive Charlie of his sleep just because I was restless; that would be so selfish as an individual, and as a leader.

Charlie was in a deep sleep and I could not deprive him of that rare feeling. I do not know why but when you are this far north completely detached from civilization and anything that even slightly resembles normal life, that sleep, when it comes, brings strange and eerie dreams. Such vivid visions of outlandish mental images. Is it because we are so tired mentally and physically? Or is it because, during the course of the day you are all alone in your own mind, cut off from the rest of the world, you enter another world.

Dreams up here are so life-like you often are unable to determine whether you have actually slept or not. Whether you are just in a trance of surreal mental suspension or an actual deep sleep, these feelings are beyond my understanding.

Who knows? I did not come to any established conclusion, even after 70 long days under the arctic stars.

This to me is a state of understanding that I find hard to categorise, for me there has to be a rational explanation to almost all that goes on in life.

As soon as I saw Charlie start to stir, I took that as my signal to make the first move and vacate my sleeping bag and start the precarious job of lighting our stove. We had a disciplined routine; that we would not cook with the sleeping bags in the tent; therefore reducing the amount of condensation that could possibly find its way into the hollow fill fibres.

This meant that in the long run the sleeping bags properties were far greater for a longer duration, than one full of moisture that would turn into sheets of ice only minutes after the body has vacated it. So Charlie knew he had little time to come around and get motivated.

I managed to light the stove, ready for Charlie to appear from his cocoon into a warm and inviting environment. The tent would fill with a radiance that was heavenly, such a comforting feeling in such unnatural conditions. Any warmth was so pleasing and mentally upraising. To keep the mind stimulated and alive was an art.

While Charlie packed both sleeping bags away in our sledges he had another look at our developing problem. Through his weary eyes I could tell we were no better off and the ice had not re-attached to firm or solid ice. So we thought, 'Oh well, let's treat today as a full rest day and not go anywhere.'

During my planning phase of this expedition I had taken great advice from some great adventurers and explorers, one being Dr David Hempleman-Adams. I recall him saying to me before we departed from base camp , 'Alan, take your time and enjoy it.' Well, now the occasion to take heed of his advice, and take our time. I had already planned that in certain stages of the journey we would take rest days, so there was already an element of flexibility incorporated into my plan. This unplanned stop just meant I had to alter my strategy a little. Not enough, though, that would cause any logistical problems.

I think the reason my plan worked and why we as a team achieved success where many others had failed, was because I had acquired knowledge and wisdom from others before I set off on a journey into the unknown, instead of setting off and then wasting time acquiring the requisite knowledge and information with limited resources.

This, I believe, is a great attribute of any leader. It shows they have the foresight not only to embrace any eventualities but they have taken into consideration the feelings and thoughts of the rest of the team. A leader must be able to think as a leader and also as a team member. This will allow him or her to make decisions based on knowledge and information from the big picture, from both sides, not just their own perspectives.

So a rest day it was. We were a little low on fuel so we used it only to melt enough ice for the relevant meal or drink and no more. We tried to sleep and rest but our bodies were so out of synch and routine that even to doze off was a luxury. We managed to consume six thousand calories, and the most physical effort would be going outside for the extremely cold action of conducting our daily motion. The day passed by and we were settling down for the night when we heard another almighty boom from what seemed directly in front of our tent door. We knew now it was no animal, it was the ice moving beneath our tent.

Imagine trying to get some sleep after watching a frightening horror movie, your mind is all over the place and focused on the worst case scenario so much that you think you are doomed to die at any given moment. Well that is the feeling we tried to sleep on. No chance. After only two hours of restlessness I dressed myself up ready to explore the immediate ice around our tent. As soon as I was fully out of the tent and had full vision my heart dropped.

The patch of ice we were on was comfortably floating towards Greenland and had just been reduced by 50 percent: we were now marooned on a buoyant ice island no larger than 40 metres wide. Alarming as it was, there was little we could do.

My patience is usually strong and I cope with most eventualities: however, there is a breaking point. Having no realistic options to combat the problem was now eating away at me. I had my hands tied. We both felt physically great after our forced rest day. Even though we had no extra sleep, just doing nothing had recharged all our strength and energy and we were ready to fight another day.

Sir Ernest Shackleton said, 'Better to be a lame donkey than a dead lion.' We had been rejuvenated and now had the energy to try and work out a scheme. I soon came up with a simple concept that eventually would form the path to our escape. Why did I just think of a solution? Was it because I had recharged my body and in turn that had recharged my thought process? Who knows? So simple was the idea, I was annoyed with myself not to have thought of it the previous night when I was tired. Maybe that is why the idea escaped me, extreme mental fatigue. Maybe my head, too, wanted a break and a rest.

I studied the direction of our drift and calculated the speed at which we were drifting. Simple time, distance and speed mathematics. By checking from the previous day and night's Global Satellite Position we had drifted nearly 400 nautical miles.

During the course of the morning I kept a record on a chart of the speed we were currently traveling at, and as soon as we slowed down it was time to put the idea and plan into action. I guessed, and that is all it was, that if we slowed down enough, the immediate fringes of broken ice would have the opportunity to re-freeze and slow this out of control ice floe right down. If it slowed down enough our adopted piece of ice may attach onto a firm, solid structure of stable ice. This would be our escape route.

This was what I planned and hoped for. We now had to play an adventure game of wit and tactics against the arctic gods. Who had the stronger nerve? It was a matter of personal motivation against Mother Nature, head-to-head. To enforce such a plan I had to convey all my conviction and self-belief to Charlie. It was going to take the two of us bonded by hope and will to escape; we needed each other's physical motivation and mental patience.

We only had one plan between us, so Charlie was all ears and liked what he heard, so a majority vote was taken and we were united in our escape to victory. The plan was so simple; once our patch of ice slowed down to a near sluggish stop and it looked likely that we could make contact with the established frozen mass, we were off it faster than a speeding bullet.

To ensure we had the optimum chance of freedom we needed to be ready to flee at a moment's notice. So how were we going to know when this moment would be? There was only one solution to this problem and if we wanted a walk to freedom enough, then we would have to find it ourselves.

Charlie and I took it in turn each hour to leave the tent and assess the floe and see where it was drifting and at what speed. If it was probable that we may attach to the frozen ocean, most of the equipment was packed away in our sledges so we would not waste valuable time when the big push came. We would take it in turn every 60 minutes to conduct this analysis. We trusted each other's judgment absolutely. We kept repeating this process every hour for two days constantly searching for that moment. It was a frustrating game of patience, however our nerves would hold out long enough to give us the edge.

The obvious problem we were encountering was one of both added mental and physical exhaustion. Once one of us had returned to the tent after 30 minutes of searching for an escape route, it would be only another 30 minutes before the other went out and tried. This meant that there was a constant bustle of either one of us getting dressed or undressed. So sleep deprivation became an added factor to hinder our escape.

We would only have the minimal amount of stores in the tent during this troubled time, so what luxuries we had, we stowed outside. We prayed for the weather to hold out and the high pressure that was with us at the moment, to stay put. My mind was growing tired of trying to preplan and stay one step ahead of the adversity. Each day wasted drifting towards Greenland brought further complications to our food and fuel supply. To combat the drift if we ever were released from this floating jail, we would have to work twice as hard to make up for lost time.

The feeling of inhuman physical exhaustion and pain soon swamped the elation of potentially escaping. Pain was in every joint and every muscle throughout the body. Who was going to win this game of frustration? My body was starting to weaken with the extreme and constant fatigue of checking for the magic moment when we could escape. I was so tired that I felt a very disagreeable cold sort of feeling, quite different from the physical chill that I normally suffered. It was a mental coldness. I also felt some resentment that we were losing sight of our true goal, or was I experiencing a conscious fear of possible death? I wasn't too sure.

I became anxious about my team and Charlie, for we had so little food left to eat and we were below the correct amount of fuel needed to see the trip through in any form of comfortable state.

'When we make it off this floating island and when we make it to the Pole I know we will have some great stories to tell.' That was going to be my opening line in tonight's diary entry if we were still beached on this tormenting ice floe. Too much time doing nothing gave the chance for all the arctic devils to chip away at your mental strength, trying to prise your consciousness and mind open and sow their seeds of doubt and poison. For our sanity's sake and for the sake of possibly our lives we needed to evacuate as soon as possible. Charlie came bursting through the tent door with a very rare smile on his face and said, 'This looks good, I think we can go.'

That was all the encouragement I needed; I trusted him with my life and that was the price of the stakes we were playing for, so let's go. We rapidly packed all the equipment and stores haphazardly into the sledges with the preconception of sorting that problem out once we were across the other side. Within five or six minutes the campsite resembled nothing more than a flattened ice rink with two indentations in the ground where we had laid. It looked no different to the patch of ice to its right or left.

Charlie led the way to the point that he deemed the strongest to cross and showed me our exit route. With a wry smile on my face I stepped onto this gangplank to freedom and galloped like an Arabian stallion, dragging all my goodly belongings with me. The dash to sanity was only ten metres long and took no longer than eight seconds.

The fact was that we had been held up for 48 hours waiting to make an eight second dash. To me, the fact was we had waited with the patience of saints to find a way forward, for two whole days. We had held our nerves long enough to give ourselves an option to succeed. Within eight seconds our dream was alive and definitely kicking again. We had won this battle, now it was time we set to and fight the rest of the war.

We both crossed and arrived safely on the other side. Safely and proudly we stood brimming with sky high self-esteem and even though there was only Charlie and me for a thousand miles, we stood with an immense feeling of self-pride and grand importance. We had been faced with one of those moments of intense emotional feeling when it seemed as if something was trying to pull you into its own vortex of mayhem. The special will or gift to rise above it and search for a workable solution is something I find fundamental to achieve, yet perplexing to understand.

I could not believe what nature then threw at us. After all we had endured nature threw a storm from Lucifer's heart, right down our throats. We walked right into a blizzard coming from Siberia with ferocious head winds dropping the temperature to below -70°C. Drastic action was essential. We set up camp and battened down all the hatches with every object we had, to try and sit the storm out. We were playing the devil at arctic roulette. The wind was so hostile and mighty it was blowing loose snow, spindrift, all around our little habitat. It was a relief being inside, but the drifting snow was building up at such great speed we religiously had to dig our way out of a potential snow grave every hour, or pay the price in a cold, frozen tomb. The many books of Sir Ernest Shackleton and Captain Scott I had read came flooding into my mind, with the image of Scott's tent turned into a wintry cairn. I did not come here to die. No journey is worth that. So each hour one of us would get fully clothed and brave the void outside to dig the tent out. When he returned to the safety and comfort of the tent it would be only half an hour before the next man replicated the same life saving ordeal. We had no rest or sleep for two days. We had to do this to give ourselves an option of a) living; and b) carrying on north to our ever-diminishing destiny.

When either nature or another force seriously threatens your life, you dig deep, deeper into your soul than you have ever dug. I had left my sweetheart Michelle in England four months' pregnant with our first son. Every minute of every day of every week, my thoughts would jump back to how Michelle was feeling. How could I have been so selfish to want to do this and risk it all, life included. We sat out the blizzard and must have removed tons of snow, but we paid the price physically. The skies cleared and morale was on a high again. We had only been walking two days and what seemed like the end of the world came upon us. First, we were hit with another savage and brutal storm. This lasted a mere eight hours but it brought with it three weeks of completely barbaric and cruel pandemonium. What happened next, nearly cost Charlie and me our lives. We ended up blind-roped together, painfully stumbling through a sea of misery and tribulation, inch by inch. Our consciousness could not become any lower and the grim reminder of second time failure and possible death overrode any motivation. The next three weeks were the ultimate trial of human, endurance, courage, vision and passion.

What we faced and conquered was the ultimate challenge man could ever fear. For three whole weeks Charlie and I could not see one hand in front of the other. We were entangled in an undiminished white out. You cannot differentiate where is left or right, up or down. It is like being one inch away from a television screen once all the programmes have finished. Sheer unadulterated torment. This was the bleakest and mentally darkest stage of the expedition. This frustration was grinding its way into our minds. Infecting each of us with a demoralizing virus to quit. We could not choose a route through the rubble. We could not walk around open water and avoid getting wet or plummeting through the ice. For the first time we had to comply with what nature threw at us. We had no options if we wanted to succeed apart from to keep moving north. The only other option was to discontinue. An option I had never allowed to invade my mind up until now. We were both extremely withdrawn and depressed. Each hour seemed like a week. The arctic devil was on our back. Would he have enough poisonous material to weaken our minds? After 14 days of falling down ice holes, stumbling into open water and covering little ground, Charlie found he had gone completely blind. I knew this was a risk because of the constant glare of ice and our eyes had refocused on a distance of one metre. I was half-blind and was vomiting all day. We had hit rock bottom physically. We camped early one night and constructed emergency pinhole goggles using the rear card in our diaries, elastic from our waistbands and surgical tape from our medical kit. This would only allow the minimum amount of UV rays onto our retinas and hopefully reduce the glare. We had to try; we had to give ourselves options. Options for victory and success. The easy and natural route would be to quit. Our food and fuel supplies were nearly gone and we still had a great deal of mileage to cover. We were exhausted both mentally and physically. We were surviving on 250 calories a day instead of the planned 6,000. I remember contacting our UK project officer Paddy George over the radio and I could tell he was conveying what seemed like the nation's concern for us. He asked in such a friendly, warming but sincere manner how we were. My instant reply was 'Paddy we are focused not blinkered -we are not taking uncalculated and foolhardy risks.' I knew that with the strength of that reply we had earned ourselves some grace. Now we had to finish the job we came out here to do.

To compound our ever-decreasing determination and hope we were now faced with a potential showstopper, the mother of despair and gloom. After all the adversity and turmoil we had faced and overcome in the previous weeks, I thought if we could battle through this three week void we had made our own luck. Our weary bodies had little energy and drive left inside them. Little physical vigour left within. We needed each other mentally now more than physically. Our bodies were emaciated beyond recognition. We had lost over 45 pounds each in body weight. I was at a weight I had not been since I was 13 years old. This was having devastating effects on both of us. Team members had plummeted through the wintry iced water, two had to be extracted for serious, potentially life threatening medical problems, we had started in complete darkness using candles and torches to search our way north, Charlie had nearly broken his back, we had to jettison vital equipment, vast pans of open water caused great delays, razor rubble had ruined our sledges, the blizzards had nearly engulfed our tent, we had lost all voice communications with the base camp , our dwindling food and fuel supply was crippling us, the indescribable three week white out drained our mental focus, what else could happen? Well... the unbelievable did.

We were now walking for 18 hours a day, trying to get the most energy from the limited amount of food. We were only consuming 250 calories a day and burning nearly nine thousand; the ratio of work to calories was frightful. We had only mental victuals left. We were now making great progress and had beaten the age-long British record of farthest north unsupported by Sir Ranulph Fiennes, and we were in grasp of the arctic grail when we approached a not common semi-frozen lead which turned into a flowing river some half a mile across and spread east and west, as far as the eye could see. Our sledges were not capable of floating. The rift was too wide, we had jettisoned all our emergency stores and we did not have the food to spend any time diverting. On top of all that, our team in the UK was now seriously worried, because we had extended our time on the ice by over a week against the plan. We thought we had made our own luck by battling through the last void and yet still we would have to be pushed into another mental dimension. However, after a few chosen four letter words we stopped and put the tent up. I knew why this had happened, because of global warming, and we now had 24 hours of sunlight, so semi-frozen water never had the opportunity to freeze. It was time for some really intricate decision-making, the most difficult yet.

We were drained from rational thought by the three-week blizzard, so to comprehend what was halting our progress dumbfounded me. I rested that night and let Charlie cook for once. On the side of the cook board I wrote out seven possible options and relayed them via weak radio to base camp . We agreed whatever action we chose we would stick by it, to the end, no matter what. In the morning we shook hands and prayed we had somehow made the right choice. 20 hours later we were still going in the wrong direction. The feeling of turning around and changing the option was killing me but we stuck to our guns. This open arctic river would not ease up, and then suddenly from nowhere there was an ice bridge that can only be described as a walkway to heaven. The bridge spanned the floe; it was two metres wide and solid enough to take our weight. We crossed in typical fashion with an almighty shout once we were safe on the other side. As soon as we touched the far bank all the clouds parted and gave us warm sunshine beaming through like golden comet tails. These would illuminate a path to victory and absolution. We had recharged with adrenaline and channelled focused drive and there was nothing now that could stop us. We had confronted it all and we stood tall. We had beaten the odds.

The last three days of the walk were spent with no food at all, just plastic bags filled with snow tied around our necks under our jackets. This would supply us with enough tepid water to keep our bodily functions going.

The Last Day Cometh

We were like two young boys waiting for Christmas day morning. The anticipation of arriving at the North Pole overpowered all our feelings of exhaustion, weariness, fatigue and the ever-increasing hunger pains. To get to the pole was all that mattered; the last 69 days were momentarily forgotten. However, we knew due to the physical state of us, we still had to stay attentive and not take any risks at such a late stage. We could not let this glowing feeling of anticipation blind us into walking on unreliable unstable ice. It only takes half a meter of wobbly weak ice for you to plummet into the Arctic Ocean we still had a few miles to negotiate!

Our routine in the tent that morning was exceptionally efficient the best it had ever been, with little to do because of the lack of food and hot drinks to prepare. We were now in a mindset of 'yesterday was the last night in the tent, this is our last morning and we have made our own luck'. We went through exactly the same routine as we had gone through the previous nine weeks; everything was packed away where it belonged, everything was double-checked, everything was just as it should be, we would not leave ourselves in such a possibly compromising position that the project would become jeopardized. Routine and mental obedience had got us this far we were so close to completion any slacking now may have catastrophic implications. The mental anchor point visualised in our minds was the top of the world (what would it look like?); this would be the sole driver now, the one thing that forces us to put one foot in front of the other when your body is crying out for you to stop and rest.

As we very wearily set off that morning, it soon became evident that we were walking on a form of adrenaline. Maybe because we knew that this was or should be our last day hauling, we suddenly became extremely weak. You would have thought that it would be the opposite being so close, but because we had endured so much over the course of nearly ten weeks we were utterly drained; our bodies were shutting down. We hadn't eaten properly or sufficiently for days now it was starting to take its toll on both of us. Our sledges weighed probably 50 kilograms by now, nearly a third of our starting weight but they seemed harder to pull then they did in the very beginning. This just exemplified our bodies' frailty and weakness. The body had depleted to such depths that we were close to collapsing. It should have been the most beautiful enjoyable miles on the journey but it turned out to be the hardest, physically mentally and emotionally. We had to carry on; the power of our belief was edging us forward towards the goal.......the Geographic North Pole.

We believed from day one that we could do this, so today is just another day we still believe we can do this albeit it was now day 70.

We could only manage one hour of hauling at a time; we were so worn-out, we were fixing on a point in the distance that was visible for what we estimated would be an hours' walk away. Judging distances and time markers over the last ten weeks had now become a well-accustomed knack. Breaking down the day into sub-targets then each sub-target into micro-targets was a way which we adopted way back in the planning and preparation of the trip, and we needed to adhere to it more than ever now because we were both physically and mentally fatigued. We soon noticed that what would normally have been our hour marker was unattainable. This gave us concern that the day was going to be far longer and more gruelling than we expected. We were walking so slowly.

After an hour of head down, arms just hanging by our sides, silent hauling we both just collapsed, laid face-up on top of our sledges so the sun could warm our face. We would both collapse and sleep until one of us would fall off the sledge and wake up or the wind would emerge from behind an ice boulder as a natural alarm clock and chill us to the point where we had to come out of what seemed a mini coma.... We were gone! Flat out, nearly unconscious to the world, to where we were, to the fact that we were quite vulnerable and lonely. Two worn-out beings floating on a frozen ice cap in the hope of attaining the arctic grail.

Each time we stopped and woke we would switch on the GPS and see how much further suffering we had to endure. This procedure repeated itself all day silent hauling, exhaustion, re-energizing snooze, wakeup call, GPS, silent hauling.

Ten miles nine miles eight miles.........I was hauling on a core conviction deep down inside me, the will to succeed the will to deliver the will to complete was being turned into physical energy, energy that seemed to come from nowhere. How long I could carry on like this was uncertain we were becoming weaker and weaker even though the final destination was becoming closer and closer. We weren't making much progress we were walking slower and slower the sledges seemed to becoming heavier and heavier.

Six miles to go……at this point in the trip I was washed out and was finding it very hard to think straight and focus on what we had to do. After five lengthy years of work, planning, training, preparing, researching and dreaming, the man who I knew the least before the trip came shining through like a bolt of lightening. Charlie was now motivating me, leading the hour's walk, encouraging both of us to carry on forward, meter by meter, mile by mile. He had found a surge of mental impetus a driving force that came from deep within him, a determination and focus that dragged both our arses towards the top of the world…The selection months back and the reasons why I chose Charlie all came clear - and true to form, the key to success was unconsciously found before we had taken one step on the frozen ocean, before Charlie had even put on a pair of skis for the first time in his life.

Charlie's stubbornness to give into himself and his tenacity and doggedness to complete the journey was a testament to his outlook on life. If he said he would deliver and perform he did. Unquestionably and absolutely; even with a smile now and again, albeit hidden behind a frozen beard of mucus, perspiration and stale porridge oats.

Even though Charlie was pushing us both forward we were still moving slowly but we were moving five miles, four miles, three miles, two miles; the actual feeling of success was starting to dawn. We were going to complete the journey even though we were shuffling along we were going to make it. The emotions started to filter into the mind and body. What will we do when we get there? How will we feel? What are we really expecting? What will we do after arriving there? Was it going to be worth the five years of dreaming? Was it going to fulfil my expectations? An influx of questions was now racing through my mind keeping it alive and animated again, now in a little daydream shuffling edging toward the pole.

GPS now said one mile…This is it the final stage; so close to standing atop of our planet earth. That one thought has always amazed me; we would be stood directly on top of the planet we live on. Quite bizarre! Charlie and I walked side by side in what seemed disbelief but contentment as we skied towards the pole. We kept looking up looking ahead as if we could bring the pole forward or make us travel faster towards what in our minds is a definitive point.

We noticed a prominent black blemish on the horizon but paid it little thought and attention as we were now fully focussed on reaching the pole. Nothing else mattered, but we couldn't shake off this dark image ahead, not far off our course hidden behind an ice boulder. It seemed like a huge black sharks fin sticking out from beneath the frozen ocean. Unbelievable, really. All we had seen for 70 days was snow and ice, blue and white; our visual sensory deprivation had been extreme, so to see a colour so divorced from our newly accustomed shades of blue and white was difficult to compute. We felt a natural draw to change course over to the enigma but we didn't; we headed off north.

The new image had engaged and ambushed our thoughts and concentration away from the now purgatory of hauling the sledges, we momentarily forgot that we were so close to reaching the Pole we stopped and quickly pressed the power button on our GPS to see how much further we had to go. We could not believe our eyes……..for the first time in ten weeks the GPS was reading south!!! Five years work, ten gruelling weeks on the ice, all the setbacks and pain, and we had missed the damn Pole. We had walked straight over the top of the world and were heading towards Siberia. Complete disbelief and a little irritation rushed over me. How could we be so foolish? So negligent? The black scar!

We simply turned about retraced our footprints GPS in hand and walked back to the North Pole. A huge sense of liberation came over me: the initial feeling was more relief, than it was elation. I lived and shattered a five year dream in that final step. 90 degrees north, top of the world, the Geographic North Pole: the emotions came flooding in. We double-checked that we were exactly there, I gave Charlie a huge hug, shook his hand and said thank you. Then we both wept for a short while until we realised our tears of relief, joy, and achievement would soon freeze our eyelashes together so we quickly stopped.

All of a sudden I became instantly cold, really cold. The body and mind had been punished enough, and the Arctic Ocean had had more than its pound of flesh from us and pushed itself far beyond the normal boundaries of endurance, sacrifice, and mental ability. It had now let go; it had delivered and wanted some rest. I turned around Charlie was suffering in the same way; we were starting to shut down physically.

We quickly took some happy snaps; some pictures at the pole, but we were so exhausted so feeble, we only managed a handful and rushed ones at that. The piece of ice, the exact point where the North Pole was marked by one of my ski poles didn't look any different than any other piece of ice we had seen over the 70 days but it meant so much.

We felt a loss while we were stood there, a loss for Paul and Jason who had battled through the first 32 days of the journey with us, a loss for Dave and

Freddie who I knew would have wanted to have been here and shared such a satisfying moment. Our sense of achievement and success was due to all the team the whole team: the squad, the support in Resolute Bay, the support in the UK, the Royal Marines, the sponsor's investors, well-wishers, friends, loved ones and family were all part of the team. Anyone who was touched by the project deserved to feel what both Charlie and I experienced at the North Pole. It was sad that only us two would personally experience that emotion.

After the few photographs were taken and we were happy that the event had been recorded sufficiently our thoughts even though we were so cold and tired turned automatically to the black scar….What on earth was it? We knew it was alien and divorced from our new surroundings and horizons but what exactly was it? After being so focused and deprived of colours and the normal infusion of bright inspiring shades of the rainbow, it had us hooked. We had to investigate; we had to find some energy and oomph to be able to answer the questions that were swirling around inside both of us.

What happened next and what we found was unbelievable!

We unclipped our harnesses and left our sledges at the Pole. I removed the shotgun from the sledge and slung it across my back and we free-skied towards our next adventure…The scar.

As we were approaching the black object our eyes were desperately trying to focus on what it was which then would tell the frozen brain and help it compute this surreal moment. We were extremely tired so the skiing was at no great pace but eventually we approached closer and closer and then the penny dropped, we both realised simultaneously that the object was an aeroplanes tail fin, protruding from behind the ice block at such an unnatural angle we knew something was extremely amiss.

We stepped over the small ice rubble wall that seemed to embody the plane's position to disbelief…As we approached the plane, we saw many sets of footprints that ran off at all angles around the plane, off to all directions of the compass. Then we saw blood spatters and small pools of blood (or so we believed) that seemed so vibrant against the white snow.

Immediately I said to Charlie, 'let's gingerly do a quick 360° search around the plane starting in opposite directions and meet back here'. Remaining on our skis to displace the weight as the ice was so thin, we headed off on a hunt for survivors or any other clues to why this plane had nose-dived into the ice breaking through the Arctic Ocean and had rested so precariously with the engine partially submerged and frozen into the sea.

As we arrived back at our starting point the clues had started to make up a picture and the realization of events had slowly started to evolve. We did not find any survivors and the plane was eerily deserted, the blood or so called blood wasn't blood at all. Mistakenly we had thought that there had been a terrible crash and some of the crew or passengers were seriously injured. The crimson trail we saw was not blood but deposits of the contents of a search and rescue flare. The crew had obviously lit a flare for a rescue plane to see them and as it was burning, the spent residue from the flare had decorated the ice with these pools and splatters of red magma. This was a relief and helped us to piece this bizarre end of the journey together. The plane we heard last night overhead which we thought was dropping fuel at the Pole for our pick-up, was this crew's rescue plane and the flare had been used to help the pilot locate them and determine the wind direction.

Knowing our HF radio batteries were knackered I very slowly edged my way onto the tilting plane and moved forward to the cockpit in hope of flicking the planes HF radio on and hopefully speaking to anyone on the other end. With my heart in my mouth I inched toward the pilots seats and looked up to see that the radio was missing. How odd! I double-checked, then the plane started to creak and groan against the ice. Momentarily my very tired life passed by as thoughts of a exceptionally cold watery grave cocooned inside an old Russian plane went fleetingly through my mind. I very gingerly crept backwards and left the plane and skied off to the edge of where it had crashed. Back with Charlie I explained what I had seen and what was missing. Charlie had stayed by the edge waiting to help me if I encountered any trouble on the plane, which was a comfort I had experienced with him many times while walking to the Pole. He was always close by just in case. We were still both bemused slightly so we now scanned the surrounding area for any further signs of the crash site. Soon Charlie dropped to his knees; he stood back up grinning like he had found some lost money. It was far more valuable what he found than any money could ever be......it was a chocolate, a Rolo, to be exact Charlie had found one solitary chocolate and it felt like we had stumbled across a secret entrance to Willy Wonka's Chocolate factory! Then another, then another; we couldn't believe it after being out of food for so long and before that, trying to survive on ever depleting rations we had struck gold.

The trail of chocolate lead to an emergency igloo, huge boulders of ice had been cut with an ice saw and made into a temporary shelter a very good one albeit.

We looked inside, in disbelief we found gallons of cooker fuel which to us meant heat and then Charlie opened a cardboard box to find fresh bread, meat, ham, cheese, crisps, beef jerkin and frozen milk…You could imagine our feeling: like two little boys waiting for Christmas last night; well, here it was. We fell to the floor still with skis attached and ate like gannets, gorging on the food until ten minutes later it hit our stomach lining and we both threw up. Too much too rich too fast too soon; but how nice the vomit tasted as it was regurgitated.

We left the igloo and had a look around: loads of mechanical tools and tarps, then we discovered a diamond…A pristine brand new beautiful black sporting shotgun in its case with all its shells. Well, boys will be boys. We loaded it up and between us fired off all the ammunition in celebration of reaching the Pole, and also just to have some fun. After nearly breaking our very weak shoulders, all the shells were spent. Our adrenaline was pumping and with our energy restored, we replaced the gun in its case as if it had never seen daylight before, as if no one would ever know.

The stricken plane was a Russian Antonov 2 from Alaska. Five experienced aviators including the famous Burt Rutan had flown to the Pole for a champagne lunch when they were forced to evacuate the plane after it sank into the ice.

Later, once we returned to Resolute Bay we learned that Burt who had been in some tight scrapes before in his life knew how hungry and depleted we were after listening to the HF conversations over the last week or so and had left the box of food for us to find. He knew we were running on empty and surviving through grit, stubbornness, determination and the will to stay alive. Gestures like that come few and far between in a lifetime. It had the same impact and meaning as Pete Goss's gesture at the very beginning when we were struggling to find the funding. Invaluable and immense emotionally to me.

My worry now was that if that plane had crashed through the ice and the ice wasn't thick enough what about our evacuation plane? Would the pilot deem that the ice was too thin too land? Would we have to walk miles to an alternative landing site? What if the plane could not extract us at all? A new influx of concern and contingency was injected into my head. There was nothing we could do now but wait. We set camp, our last camp we hoped, on some stable ice next to the igloo and anchored the tent down as per normal just in case a freak wind picked up and started to blow the tent away. We were all set for our party at the Pole, with our last shot of Johnnie Walker Whisky, as promised to Johnnie Walker. We would toast them and Black Label at the top of the world as we had done; every degree north latitude we had crossed on the journey.

Our home, the tent was ready for the last supper, with our newly found box of goodies and enough fuel to have a sauna. We had reached the Pole, now we had to wait. As soon as we had placed the last ice block against the skirt of the tent we heard an engine in the far distance. It couldn't be? Could it? We waited outside on the ice and then into view came the tiny little dot of our freedom bird…The plane, our plane, but so soon.

After five years work and ten weeks of hauling I wanted to spend a night at the top of the world. You would wouldn't you after all that? But it was not meant to be. A little disappointed but relieved, we couldn't have asked for any more from Freddie and the team in Resolute Bay. They timed our pick-up to perfection knowing what state we were in they knew we needed extracted as soon as possible and had launched the pane the previous day. What virtual understanding and teamwork.

Within ten minutes our plane landed only feet away form our tent. As it taxied the lovely pilot Amy shouted out the window: *'guys you have 20 minutes otherwise you are walking home'*. That was final.

She had seen the ice conditions as she circled looking for a place to land and had seen all the ice breaking up so with this information, plus the very visual reminder of the sinking plane, her decision was final…Who were we to argue?

We quickly packed all our equipment away and managed a Sky news interview, some pictures, a small bottle of champagne, and read some congratulatory letters too. As we were celebrating, the crew were hand-pumping some barrels of fuel into the plane so we could be flown back to civilization. It was disappointing to learn that Dave, Paul and Freddie were not on the plane as promised as I wanted all of us to reach the Pole, but it was the pilot's call, and due to the increased weight of three extra packs, Amy could not afford to take the chance so unfortunately they had to wait in Resolute Bay for us to be re-united.

As we taxied and then took off we were soon airborne the crew handed both of us a beer (a pint of Guinness would have been nice) and we sat near the cockpit which was the warmest part of the plane.

It became very apparent very quickly that we had not had a wash for ten weeks. The warm air from the engine soon fanned our very putrid bodies and clothing and soon the whole plane managed to taste us!

It wasn't long before Charlie was asleep as the combination of success, extreme fatigue, relief, warm air and a beer took its toll. I stayed awake purposely to reflect on the journey. I stared out of the small window looking at the ice and the frozen ocean beneath us that we had walked on. From the bird's eye view I noticed that our path to the Pole was always one step ahead of the ice breaking up. We had beaten the odds, we had walked on water, had achieved the impossible. It was a nice feeling inside of contentment that we were always one step ahead, that was due to the passionate planning understanding awareness and respect of the challenge and environment we chose to put our selves in and on.

What took us 70 days to walk across took the plane seven hours to fly across. Once we had left the ocean and started to fly over the mountain range at Ward Hunt I went to asleep. The dream over, against the odds we had delivered…What next?

For me, leadership means you have to hold values such as being innovative, versatile and resilient with a strong emphasis on accountability for others and performance, along with the ability to alter your strategy and give your team options to pursue your goal.

On reaching the North Pole Alan and Charlie had pitched a tent and had hoped to spend the night there, relishing the achievement. Their relief plane landed within hours of their success to extract them and take them to safety. Alan describes a feeling of frustration at this point but on reflection he realized that this was according to the pre-agreed plan and was in the ultimate interest of their safety. The support team, vital to the ultimate success of the expedition, were doing their job. Once the word was out that they had succeeded the plaudits flowed and were most emotionally appreciated.

A letter was sent from all the heads of the British forces, the Royal Marines, Royal Navy, the Army and the Royal Air Force.

Upon release of the news the Houses of Parliament interrupted it activity, an announcement of the success was made and an early morning motion of congratulation and recognition was signed by 143 Members of Parliament.

That great British explorer, Sir Ranulph Fiennes, wrote a letter which was faxed to Alan and Charlie:

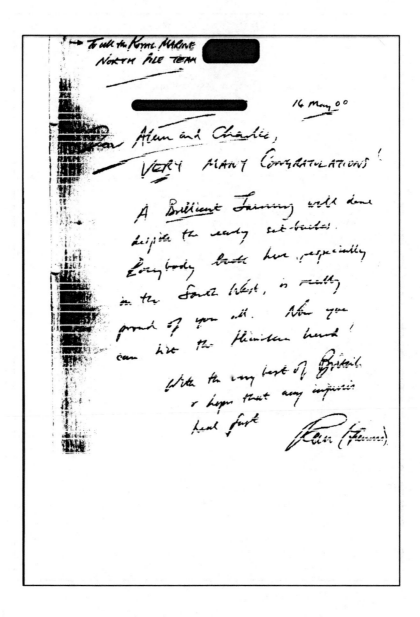

A telegram was received from Buckingham Palace:

ROYAL COURT TELEGRAM

TO: CORPORAL ALAN CHAMBERS AND MARINE CHARLIE PATON

FROM: H.R.H. THE DUKE OF EDINBURGH

MANY CONGRATULATIONS ON YOUR FANTASTIC ACHIEVEMENT WHICH REFLECTS VERY WELL ON YOU, YOUR TEAM AND THE CORPS.

PHILIP

CAPTAIN GENERAL

Please despatch immediately

THURSDAY, 18TH MAY, 2000

---

4 - Team Polar 2000 Post Expedition Review

by Alan Chambers

In this chapter we provide the post expedition review which was drawn up by Alan Chambers shortly after the successful Team Polar 2000 expedition This is in the main unedited and provides details of the setup, planning, training, execution and review of the expedition. As the expedition was conducted from within the Royal Marines it is written primarily as a military document and is of benefit for future polar adventurers and expeditions. The Appendices include more detail as follows:

Appendix I - Glossary of terms

Appendix II - Overview of Key Stages of Team Polar 2000 Expedition

Appendix III - Scheme of Manoeuvre by Ice Party of Team Polar 2000 Expedition

Appendix IV- Equipment List for Team Polar 2000 Expedition and Evaluation of Effectiveness

Appendix V - Selected Diary Entries of Alan Chambers – Team Polar 2000 Expedition

TEAM POLAR 2000 (TP2K)

EXPEDITION LEADER
ALAN W CHAMBERS MBE, REPORT AUTHOR

EXPEDITION PATRONS
ADMIRAL SIR MICHAEL BOYCE GCB OBE ADC
MAJOR GENERAL RHG FULTON CGRM

DR DAVID HEMPLEMAN-ADAMS OBE MBE

PROJECT OFFICER
LIEUTENANT COLONEL P D GEORGE OBE ROYAL MARINES

THE FIRST BRITISH *UNSUPPORTED* WALK FROM CANADA TO

THE GEOGRAPHIC NORTH POLE

THE GEOGRAPHICAL NORTH POLE

Planet earth spins and rotates around its axis each and every 24 hours. Where the axis meets the earth's surface is 90 degrees, position 90°. This is known as the Geographical North Pole. The Geographical North Pole lies 472 nautical miles north of Ward Hunt Island, off the tip of Ellesmere Island, Canadian High Arctic. No British team had yet been able to succeed in walking to the Pole from the Canadian coastline, totally unsupported. Unsupported means having no external help and support along the way. No food caches, dog teams, air re-supplies, over-snow vehicles, or relay teams.

AIM

To reach the Geographical North Pole (GNP), from the Canadian coastline. In essence we would start *unsupported* with a contingency to carry on forward *supported* if the eventuality arose. A simple, focused, positive aim that would not alter during the course of the walk.

ORGANISATION AND PLANNING

CONCEPT

To succeed in placing a team of Royal Marines at the top of the world, I needed to gain permission to plan, request volunteers, select the optimum team, train both physically and mentally as a team for eight months, fundraise to enable us to have the best possible equipment and support available, plan and execute the walk as a leader.   Our plan enabled us to remain flexible but focused.

SPONSORING OFFICER

LT COL PD GEORGE OBE ROYAL MARINES
COMMANDING OFFICER, COMMANDO TRAINING CENTRE ROYAL MARINES (CTCRM)

The team leader should be the initiator of the expedition regardless of rank as it was found in the case of TP2K that as always the vision and plan was in my mind, and that plan came out during team discussions and was then discussed with the team. However, all their own views and ideas for the final plan were always considered. The Major Expeditions Committee (MEC) based in Headquarters Royal Marines Whale Island, deemed an expedition of this magnitude would require the presence of a sponsoring officer. This enabled myself and the team to have a wealth of knowledge and experience when dealing with the many different aspects and departments relevant to adventure training and extreme expeditions. Not only was Lt Col George an excellent sounding board for me as a leader, he also proved to be an exceptional ambassador to TP2Kand the Corps. As sponsoring officer he was available to oversee the finance strategy and the delicate planning needed. Knowledge, wisdom, and a genuine interest in the expedition relieved some of the pressure from the team and therefore me. We could concentrate on building strength as a team. Without the support from Lt Col George we would have been tied into long correspondences to many departments within the Corps.

TEAM SELECTION & ISOLATION

The great way to solve arduous and difficult problems is to attack each situation as a team. I knew even with all the will and passion in the world I could not drag four people to the North Pole. My aim from the beginning was to succeed as a team. The training already programmed into us as Royal Marines gave us the edge.

Why hadn't any British team succeeded? We were already one step above all the other teams from many different nations. In essence half of the team building had already been done in 30 weeks of recruit training. It was now my job as a leader to instil my dream and passion into the team.

I requested volunteers in Spring 1999 on Daily Routine Orders in every regular Royal Marines establishment. One stipulation from the MEC was that I take a marine with less than two years' service. I also needed a signals communicator and the remainder of the team to be AWT. After a two month wait for returns I had the disappointment to receive only seven possible volunteers from which I needed five.

I planned to take four people on the ice and have two in base-camp, one of which would act as a reserve walker. I did the initial team selection through a seven-page questionnaire, which I distributed on receiving an application form requesting to join the team. The PT troop at CTCRM provided valuable advice and assistance in the formulation of the questionnaire.

I knew I would only have one person as wastage and would not pick the final team until we were in base camp , Resolute Bay. Unsupported is the hardest way to walk to any Pole or reach any distant goal. It needed to be a serious attempt as I had already failed in 1998. To achieve the required standard I needed my team to be in one place away from normal unit life, away from unit commitments so we could dedicate six days a week, 12 hours a day to the task in hand.

40 Commando was the preferred option as it was my parent unit and in an ideal location for travelling. Fortunately, the unit was away on operational duty, which gave us the chance of setting up office in the Education Centre. From there we were fully independent with our own transport on loan from RNAS Yeovilton, our own communications system including e-mail, mobile phone, fax and web page. Being isolated on Norton Manor Camp gave me the ideal opportunity to train, assess, and work the team for eight months prior to departure.

The conclusion of four training evolutions located in North Wales, North Scotland, Iceland and Canada resulted in the following team appointments:

ICE PARTY

Expedition Leader:	Corporal Alan Chambers 40 CDORM
Communications Manager:	Corporal Jason Garland 40 CDORM
Physical Trainer:	Corporal Paul Jones 45 CDORM
Navigational Co-Ordinator:	Marine Charlie Paton FPRMG

BASE CAMP

Base Camp Manager:	Corporal Freddie Warwick 45 CDORM
Reserve Walker:	Marine Dave Fox JSU NORTHWOOD

Team Polar 2000 (TP2K) is exactly what it states, a team. The above team members are the tip of the iceberg; since the expedition was born we have had a legion of workers all combining together to aid in the planning and preparation of the expedition. Each person who donated advice, equipment, support, funds, guidance, and encouragement has contributed to the success of the project. The success is to be reaped by every single person who helped and believed in the team.

The six that went to Canada were the privileged few that were given the chance of achieving the impossible. Just the opportunity to do so is a great inspiration and stimulus for everyone and anyone to develop their inner vision, inner passions and inner strengths. There is no room for an individual within a team.

FINANCE PROCUREMENT & CONTROL

The total budget for the expedition was to be £101K. This would cover the pre administration fees, pre-training expeditions and the main trip in its entirety. Not only was the expedition fully funded, we incorporated enough monies in the budget for a re-supply of manpower food or equipment in case of any misfortune. Safety was paramount, so funds were built in at the start to ensure practical possible contingency plans.

The three key areas we looked at to procure the funds were:

     a.   Civilian fundraiser who would generate the necessary capital.

     b.   Service funds through out the Royal Navy & Royal Marines.

     c.   Global corporate sponsorship.

We managed to obtain funds from all three key areas, with different levels of success. It was a difficult time for the Marines to warrant an expedition to the far north considering we had no manpower in northern Norway that year. IPT based at CTCRM, provided invaluable advice on procuring money from RN/RM Sports and AT funds. However, as a team we had to resource the bulk of the funding required from global corporate funds. We managed to raise corporate funds from six key companies: Johnnie Walker (Diageo), E-fax.com, The Sun newsgroup, Leeds & Holbeck Building Society, Mckinney Rogers International and DXM Ltd.

The control over the funds was always in the hands of the expedition leader. He would be the one with the big picture idea and would be able to constantly re-evaluate the budget. Alongside the leader, the project officer and also HQRM closely maintained the funds. A simple but effective book keeping system was incorporated and used throughout the trip, validated by the CPRO at HQRM.

Monies to be used in Canada, the host country, were electronically wired across the world to be in place once the team were in situ. This was a great help to the base camp party as they were dealing with the bank on a daily basis and kept control of the funds until the expedition leader returned off the ice.

It was extremely important that one of the base camp and one of the ice party were able to manage the funds independently.

INSURANCE

The British Mountaineering Council is an excellent source of insurance for any land-based expeditions. Insurance should be controlled by a base camp or rear link representative as it can be utilized ASAP should the need arise.

BASE OFFICE REQUIREMENTS

Success in a project like TP2K is founded on teamwork. The base foundation of a strong and honest team is continuity and self-belief. As a leader these qualities were paramount to the success, and also once on the ice, the safety of the team. After volunteers were identified the next step was to house the team centrally and build the nucleus to a high performance team. The Corps Drafting Officer and the project officer helped this. The last team member joined the team at Norton Manor Camp four months prior to departure. The majority of the team had been working together six months prior to the walk.

There is no doubt in my mind as the coordinator/leader that we had a great head start above our "arctic contemporaries" because we built a strong team in advance.

The office was self-sufficient in the way of telephones, (both landline and mobile) facsimile machine, Internet and e-mail, four computers and two printers, a scanner and a store room area. This was all encased within the Education Department at Norton Manor Camp. Security had to be established at a very early date not only for the IT items but we soon built up supplies of expensive, special - to - purpose outdoors clothing.

The team was in constant negotiation with directors from respective corporate companies. It was essential that the companies we approached could contact the team direct as an exchange telephone system often antagonizes the possible deal. To be able to be in direct constant communication with the world made the running of the expedition more efficient.

RESULTS & RECOMMENDATIONS
- Clear generic aim, no hidden agendas
- A project officer who has the necessary time and genuine interest to effectively contribute to the team and the overall planning.
- Liaison with the PT branch to orchestrate the team physical selection process.
- Early contact with IPT CTCRM reference time lines for all service funds to approach.
- Team transport
- Team mobile phone
- Sufficient IT appliances
- Self supporting office / store room
- Direct communications
- Use of host unit mail office and postage. Possible account with the UPO.

TRAINING

CONCEPT

To walk 472 nautical miles dragging 250 pounds of stores per man requires both great mental and physical fitness, plus stamina. With a firm base line already achieved through troop PT the team were already quite fit. It was my aim to build the individual members into a disciplined and highly motivated team, partly through our training programme.

PHYSICAL TRAINING PROGRAMME

Sgt Sylvester devised the training programme from the Physical Training branch at CTCRM. A brief outline about the expedition provided him with the general idea therefore he could sum up the physical and mental task ahead. From here more emphasis was concentrated on endurance and teamwork within the programme.

After the training program was finished Sgt Sylvester requested for Cpl Jones visit the PT branch and run through the 16-week programme. This had many benefits both for the team and also the author of the programme. It soon became apparent that the training programme would have to remain flexible due to the build-up of the team's enormous commitments.

This proved very successful and was a must, because some of the equipment required had to be signed out and loaned from the Physical Training store at CTCRM, and also the team had to procure specialized training equipment from Power-Sport, which is a sports company based in Wales. They loaned the team, special-to-purpose fitness machines, which were delivered and erected in the gym at 40 CDO RM.

EXERCISE REGIME

WEEKS 1-6

- Concentrated on building up the muscles and strength within the legs, in turn this gave a good strong base platform for the following endurance programme.

WEEKS 6-12

- Concentrated on mainly endurance work but still focusing on muscle and strength use as well.

WEEKS 12-16

- Concentrated on long and hard endurance work.

In summary, the programme worked very well, but towards the end more emphasis should have been placed on subsequent, longer endurance work.

For example:

- Longer runs incorporating different body weight exercises
- Hauling pulling more weight for shorter periods 4-6 hrs, 6-8 hrs
- Hauling pulling less weight for extended periods 8-10 hrs, 10-12hrs

Other evolutions that were incorporated into the programme were teamwork and bonding packages in Wales and Scotland. This was very beneficial and cost effective using joint service training establishments and facilities.

The locations further added to the profile of the expedition and the Corps, by incorporating national media facilities on each occasion arranged through the Corps PR staff.

WALES TRAINING PACKAGE

Occurring in 1999, this was of great benefit to the team because of the cold weather experienced and also the concentrated time away from the office working directly as a team. Once we started training on Mt. Snowdon and the immediate vicinity we endured (with wind chill) temperatures as low as -30°C.

This gave everyone just a small taste of what was to come, plus an important lesson was learnt how to keep sweating to a minimum in the cold weather. A lesson later proved a great defence against cold weather injuries when walking on the pack ice, due to the dangers of hypothermia and potential frostbite and the unconventional but essential drill of having to dry your clothes during the night.

Other arduous training involved pulling vehicle tyres for long periods and distances on the local sand dunes. These periods were outstanding and the quality training time was an exceptional insight for the task in hand, because of the resistance provided by the sand. This added a touch of realism, replicating the drag and pull of fully laden sledges on ice and snow.

Wales proved to be an excellent PR location and opportunity for the national press. The team spent a whole day conducting press photographs and interviews to add to the profile and the arduous nature of the expedition. It also proved a superb chance for real time photographs to be used on the expedition web page.

SCOTLAND TRAINING PACKAGE

Based in 2000 this again proved beneficial due to the cold weather experienced. Teamwork and mental stamina training was the main objective, as we had a sledge weighing in excess of 300 pounds.

The team training was based around manoeuvring the sled across mountainous and demanding terrain including crossing rivers and gorges. On several occasions this involved all four members of the team carrying the sled on their shoulders over major obstacles.

Whilst training in Scotland we were fortunate enough to find that we practiced a procedure that we put into effect many times during the actual expedition. Two team members would harness onto one sledge with the other two team members pushing from the rear-this later enabled the team to scale the pressure ridges encountered which ranged from 10-50ft in height and varied in width and depth. In short, the lessons learned in Scotland from the training package became an everyday occurrence once on the pack ice of northern Canada.

Once more we integrated the training with a press facility working from the joint service lodge at Rothiemurchus. Again we managed to gain national press coverage prior to our departure to Canada without compromising our aims and objectives for that particular training phase.

RESULTS & RECOMMENDATIONS

- Overall the training exercises involved in the build up to the expedition proved to be thorough and well planned out. The basic level of fitness was at a reasonably high standard with all members of the team, due to the fact we were all serving members of the Corps.

- From our own personal experiences the training packages in Wales and Scotland were essential and longer periods should have been spent in both of the aforementioned areas. This would have required further funding to stay for longer periods of time.

- Some aspects of the physical training program were purposely omitted because we wanted to peak at our top level of fitness on week four of the expedition. This was due to the fact we did not want to over train and burn out at the earlier stages rather than the latter stages on the pack ice.

- On reflection, the training programme was an excellent guide for the team to train against. Individual exercises were allocated for direct work on specific muscle groups that would be constantly in use for 15 hours a day for 10 weeks.

- A possible solution to team training would have been to mirror either a ML2 North Wales package or use the infrastructure of an NSSC in Norway to conduct winter pre training.

FEEDING / RATION SUPPORT

CONCEPT

The food had to enable the team to spend ten weeks on the pack–ice enduring extreme low temperatures, conducting physical activities for up to 18 hours a day. The estimated calorific output for an individual was 10,000 calories per day. We wanted to have a serious attempt at the Pole therefore we reduced the weight by having a staggered approach to the amount of calories consumed.

With a serious expedition such as an unsupported walk to the Geographical North Pole (GNP), nutrition is a significant consideration alongside every other aspect involved in the trip. With the expenditure of up to 10,000 calories a day through hard hauling, the choice of menu is crucial, ensuring you have all aspects of the diet covered from fats to vitamins.

As well as this, it all needs to be lightweight with high calorific values. A target of 1,000g of food per man per day was set. Previous attempts by other polar teams in these adverse conditions show that a reversal in food content is required with a resulting balance in the region of 60% fat, 32% carbohydrate and 8% protein. With a higher calorific value to gram ratio, fat is nearly three times as heavy as carbohydrates.

Therefore, against previous polar teams and nutritionists' advice, we opted for our own choice of a lightweight carbohydrate diet, which proved more worthwhile in the long run. In order to sustain each walker for a period of 60 days, considerable research was conducted into the most valuable nutritional diet possible. Advice was sought from DGST (N) Bath, and a nutritional lecturer at Warwickshire University.

The end result provided TP2K with a choice of four meals that gradually increased in calorific value from 3,000cals to 6,500cals per day per man, and weighed a little over 1,000g.

SUPPLY

With the Ministry of Defence researching a completely new ration system during the preparation phase of the expedition we extracted vital findings from ongoing research. The new patrol ration, which was soon to be infiltrated into the services, held the basis of our daily food intake. We contacted DGST (N) Ensleigh, Bath who invited us to test and taste the new ration system. This proved extremely beneficial and rewarding. From there we had to identify how and where we could procure the rations. Major Jim Reed the Corps Catering Officer housed at CTCRM, provided the team with enough patrol rations for training and for the main trip. We supplemented the necessary excess rations for re-supply and for training in Canada from 22 SAS Headquarters Hereford. With these kind donations, we had nearly all the food we required.

To supplement the rations with further carbohydrates, we contacted High Five Ltd who donated, at a reduced cost, all the power bars and supplement drinks. These were a critical part of the development of the team's physical condition. We started to consume the power bars and drinks during the last three months of our time in UK.

PACKAGING

Once the main daily ration plan had been identified and we were in possession of all the necessary food supplements, we split the food into manageable groups. All unnecessary outer packaging was removed. This helped reduce the overall weight over the 70 days.

We devised a system of how we wanted to pack the food in the sledges. Each team member's sledge had to replicate the team leader's sledge. This was for easy access; once we were static any person could enter any sledge and grab a certain piece of equipment in the minimal time.

All rations were broken down into 'man-day packs' and taken out of all individual wrappers and protected in 'day bags'; this also had the advantage of preventing struggling out on the ice with five pairs of mittens on. Snack-packs were also broken into bite-sized pieces for ease when we stopped for our breaks.

The rest of the equipment in the sledge was also colour coded in lightweight stuff sacs, each team member having the same items in the same bags.

DAILY PROGRAMME

The TP2K routine was to have a hot chocolate drink first thing in the morning, which would help our daily bowel movement. We would then have porridge along with a high-energy drink. Throughout the day we would stop every couple of hours for a maximum of five minutes to consume some of our 'Snack-Pack' and hot energy drink. The intention was to get one litre of fluid intake on each break, at the end of each day we would get a fluid replacement drink, along with another main meal. On every fifth day there was the delicacy of a pudding! Later on in the evening we would have another hot chocolate, high in calories.

The longer the days hauling, the longer in time it would be between each break. To this end chunks of energy bars were kept in small specially designed pockets on the sleeve. These could then be easily retrieved and consumed whilst still walking. Only one flask at a time was ever opened, this would effectively increase the life of the other seven flasks (two flasks per walker was standard).

MEALS

As noted above the trial patrol rations supplied by DGST (N) Bath were exciting, with four new flavours including 'Pasta Carbonara, 'Chicken Balti', 'Mashed Potato, Beef-Strips' and 'Chicken Noodles'. All included a high calorific value and a plentiful supply of carbohydrates, and along with the main meals there were four new puddings, which we were to treat ourselves with on every fifth day.

However, with the sledges packed in Canada, they were extremely heavy and we had to dispose of extra weight, so the puddings had to go, as did the Apple Flakes from each breakfast. This enabled the starting sledge weight to average 244 pounds per man.

The 'Snack-Packs' was made up from brown biscuits from the ration packs; they were extremely light-weight and again high in calories. We also had great-tasting energy bars filled with simple complex carbohydrates, for both fast and long lasting energy.

Another food supply was the new *High5 Protein Bar*, which is ideal for post-exercise recovery; these were all fantastic with many different flavours. As the calories increased we added Pork Scratchings, again these are extremely lightweight and high in calories.

For the last stage we had a mixture of nuts, which would hopefully keep us going, but when we were struggling with too much weight to carry, the heavy bags of nuts were discarded.

SUMMARY

BREAKFAST

ITEM	WEIGHT (GRAMS)	CALORIES
Chocolate drink	65	228
Hot Cereal Start	100	370
Porridge Oats	70	393
Apple Flakes	35	320

SNACKS

ITEM	WEIGHT (GRAMS)	CALORIES
Biscuit Brown	84	332
Chocolate Bar	55	400
Chocolate Bar 2	60	315
H5 Energy Bar	50	194
H5 Protein Bar	60	189
Pork Scratchings	40	280

DRINKS

ITEM	WEIGHT (GRAMS)	CALORIES
H5 Energy Source	60	163
H5 Isotonic	60	220

MAIN MEALS

ITEM	WEIGHT (GRAMS)	CALORIES
Pasta Carbonara	100	412
Chicken Noodle	100	350
Potato & Beef	100	350
Chicken Balti	100	350

Even though the team consumed 254,000 calories per person over the 70 days, the Pole pair lost between 42 and 46 pounds each. This equates to 25% of their body weight. This was mainly due to the high carbohydrate diet. We purposely chose this way to give us the sustained continuous energy.

After 30 days' hauling we had already lost all our own body fat and started to burn away at the muscles beneath. This did reduce our resilience to the cold, especially below -40°C with wind chill.

RESULTS AND RECOMMENDATIONS

- The rations performed extremely well with only minor complaints on the menu plan.

- Breakfast: The porridge and hot cereal mix was an ideal breakfast, however the first three weeks on 3,000 calories, one and a half packets of cereal felt insufficient - two packets would have been better along with some dried fruit to help sustain energy levels.

- Fluids: The team drank sufficient levels of fluids throughout the expedition. Sometimes it was not possible to get one whole litre of fluid at break-times, when due to extreme cold weather the rest stops were kept to the minimum. At the end of the day in the tent what we had not consumed throughout the day we would drink in the evening. This way we kept ourselves hydrated. At any time, if we had extra water in the pan after cooking our meals we always put it to good use by having more drinks. The *High5 Isotonic Drink* was fantastic after a hard day on the ice hauling a sledge.

- Snack Packs: These were good in taste and quantity, in the first couple of weeks it felt that an extra energy bar would have helped us that little bit more through the day; in future a light-weight, high fat snack i.e. Pork Scratchings would be great for cutting weight down.

- Soup: Could be an alternative in the flask throughout the day.

- Mixed nuts: Would be a great snack but for an unsupported attempt they are too heavy.

- Halvah: Was to be taken as a snack bar. Full of glucose, it's a favourite with some the arctic walkers. The taste is a required one, and we chose to leave it well alone!

- Spices: [powdered] could easily be added beforehand to the main meals to give more taste.

- Reducing the overall weight of the food is always a recommendation.

COMMUNICATIONS

CONCEPT

With any serious unsupported attempt at the GNP the weight, size and robustness of all communications equipment is paramount for a successful and safe conclusion.

Throughout the planning and preparation of TP2K, the above was taken into consideration to ensure the ice party was able to communicate 24 hours a day with the base camp by some means. Not only did this give all parties peace of mind but maintained a crucial safety link in the most inhospitable environment on earth. The composition of the Safety Emergency Plan and the overall communications projection was endorsed by WO2 A Keir Yeomen of Signals, 3 Cdo Bde RM.

SAFETY EMERGENCY PLAN

To provide a multi layered, fail-safe communications support for TP2K, encompassing all the integral communication equipment, a Safety Emergency Plan (SEP) was produced. The SEP was a four-tier plan working through flow diagram levels to ensure that the safety of the ice party was not compromised at any time. The ice party, base camp and all in receipt of the exercise instructions were familiar with the SEP.

E-MAIL

E-mail was the lifeline between the ice party and base camp. From activation, co-ordinates of the ARGOS (see below) were continually e-mailed to the base camp from the ARGOS Ground monitoring stations in the US and France. This enabled an accurate plot to be taken of the ice party as well as pre-coded messages to be transmitted.

On arrival at the original base camp facility we were unable to establish a usable telephone line to allow 24/7 access to the Internet. After four days of attempting to resolve this problem and working directly with our Internet Service Provider (Eclipse) in the UK, the problem persisted. With the safety of the ice party at risk an alternative base camp location was found that would supply us with the constant ability to communicate via email and the Internet. The South Camp Inn located in the Hamlet had an established Internet link, direct by satellite, to an ISP in Yellowknife.

However this meant that this ISP could only receive messages from our UK ISP and not transmit using our original Eclipse address of info@teampolar2000.co.uk. A Hotmail account was set up and all persons concerned were informed of the new address. This then allowed two-way traffic to flow. Our original address continued to be active, receiving the constant positions transmitted by the ARGOS.

Not only was the e-mail facility paramount for the safety of the ice party, it provided the Base camp a media link. On receipt of regular situation reports (sitrep) from the ice party, ARGOS positions and pre-coded messages, the base camp was able to generate a weekly sitrep.

The sitrep was e-mailed to HQRM where information was then disseminated to the respective press and sponsors to keep the media ball rolling. Sitreps assisted eFax.com to maintain our web site that was updated on a daily basis. Anyone surfing the net was able to send the team messages via fax, email or voice. These were then filtered by eFax.com and forwarded on to the base camp and ice party respectively. Information supplied by the base camp also assisted McKinney Rogers International in producing a regular newsletter that was mailed to VIP's, sponsors and family/friends of the team.

MAGELLAN GSC 100

During the planning stages of the expedition a great deal of research went into identifying an alternative form of communication to HF voice. With the Iridium Telephone Network announcing bankruptcy, a lightweight e-mail facility was identified. The Magellan GSC 100 is a hand-held GPS and computer enabling simple e-mail to be transmitted and received via satellites a ground station and ISP.

Working closely with Orbcomm Ireland (Orbcomm being the satellite system used by the GSC100) software data suggested that a unit would work at high latitudes. A unit was purchased from Canada and tested prior to deploying to the Canadian High Arctic. Because the unit only housed a re-chargeable battery, an alternative power source had to be made. With a voltage range of 10 – 30 Volts DC a 10 x 1.5V battery pack was procured and connected to the unit using the multipurpose cable supplied with the unit. This enabled us to use lithium AA batteries and solar panels.

On location in Resolute Bay and after ten days of attempting to communicate using the unit with assurances from Magellan and Orbcomm that the unit would work, we were unable to maintain communications using e-mail facility. The Magellan GSC 100 was not programmed into the SEP and due to the inefficient level of communication the team decided that the ice party would not take the unit.

Information can be found on the Magellan GSC 100 at: www.magellan.com or www.orbcomm.net

ARGOS was the primary form of communication between the ice party and base camp. From the day of activation the ARGOS emitted a signal identifying the location, temperature and a number of the 16 pre-coded messages. The signal would be received via satellite by a ground monitoring station that would then email the data direct to the base camp. .

The unit was rented from North American CLS, Maryland, USA. The unit was tested before delivery to TP2K. It was then tested again prior to the deployment of the ice party. Information on the ARGOS can be found at www.argosinc. com

HIGH FREQUENCY (HF) COMMUNICATIONS

There are many high frequency radios produced for expedition use. One radio, however, stands out from all the others. The Spielsbury SBX-11A. Unfortunately, Spielsbury was bought by Racal who stopped producing the set. It is commonly found in the high arctic and is renowned for its reliability and robustness by the native people. Many of the sets available today may have superior power output to the Spielsbury's 8-10W but are extremely fragile and temperamental in extreme climatic conditions.

A decision was made by the team to take the Spielsbury SBX-11A. A radio was rented and shipped from Canada enabling the team to become familiar with it.

A communications trial was set up using the USMC Base, Keflavik, Iceland. Half of the team deployed to Iceland, leaving the remainder in Norton Manor Camp. Using the assistance of STCICS, RAF Bampton Castle and Kinloss, communications were established between STCICS and Iceland using the Spielsbury. The trial enabled the team to put trust and confidence in the equipment.

A dipole (and spare) was constructed of Black/Brown wire. The length of the antenna was altered to the respective frequencies (four dedicated) by using Clansman formers. Elevation of the dipole was achieved by binding skis and ski poles together using toe straps. It was then connected to the set using bullet and spade connections. A 15Volt lithium battery supplied by Bristol Batteries, Swindon, produced the power source for the radio. It was connected to the radio using audio male/female plugs. This would allow the battery to be disconnected and kept warm prior to use

HF communications throughout the expedition were unreliable due to problems with the aural zone and a high level of solar spot activity as the sun reached the peak of its 11-year cycle in February/March this year. Frequency prediction data was received from 81 Signals Unit RAF, enabling schedules to be established between the ice party and base camp; however, persistence and perseverance became the name of the game. On one occasion the ice party was unable to establish communications with the Base camp for a period of ten days. Early on the eleventh day the frequency fell back in again and communications were established with base camp. After the early stage communications improved a little, this may have been due to the reduced activity of the sun and influx of geomagnetic storms hitting the polar region.

Throughout TP2K, 81 Signals Unit RAF, STCICS supported the ice party. Schedules were set up to allow the ice party to speak, using a telephone patch, to relatives and sponsors. The ice party was able to receive STCICS but the lack of transmission power and difficult atmospheric conditions disabled the ice party's ability to talk back.

Once communications were established, the ice party could transmit a weekly sitrep. The sitrep was devised to reduce the transmission time, thus conserving battery power and it took the form of coded crib cards. This proved to be an effective way to relay information from the ice party to base camp accurately, efficiently and with some form of privacy. This information would then be added to the final situation report that was emailed to rear link UK.

The base camp used a HF ICOM base station with dipole antenna located at First Air operations room, near the airport, this being by far the most reliable communications suite in Resolute Bay. Also in the event that communications could not be established direct with Base camp, if a First Air Aircraft was airborne at the time, it would act as a relay station back to the operations room.

EMERGENCY COMMUNICATIONS

The primary form of emergency communications was the ARGOS. However, the team leader wore close to his skin the Breitling Emergency Watch. Not only is this a stylish timepiece, but also it provides the wearer with an Emergency Locating Transmitter which, when activated, would transmit a signal on 121.5MHz. The Breitling Emergency Watch provided the ice party with a back up to the ARGOS and was on loan from Breitling.

In addition to the Breitling Emergency Watch a SARBE 5, loaned from RM Poole was taken. Only activated in an emergency, the SARBE 5 provided the ice party with an alternative emergency transmitter. When activated, the SARBE would transmit a signal on 243MHz.

The SARBE 5, along with a spare battery, GPS and spare AA batteries were vacuum-sealed and became know as the Emergency Safety Pack. Vacuum-sealed by Remploy, Glasgow (the company that vacuum seals the MOD NBC Suit) it would remain untouched except in the event of an emergency and sealed in plastic would prevent cross contamination by fuel.

In the early stages through the pressure ridge zone, all the communications equipment other than the Breitling Emergency Watch was carried in a day sack on the back of one of the walkers. This would prevent damage to the equipment in extremely low temperatures.

BASE CAMP TELEPHONES

The base camp duo had to be self-sufficient with an outside line. The manager of the base camp facility ensured that we were able to take incoming calls on all of the hostel's phones. We were also offered the facility of a facsimile machine. With this and the e-mail we were kept in constant direct contact with the UK and all our sponsors. A record of phone calls had to be itemized apart from the daily running of the hotel. We were given our own direct outside international phone line. At no time was the base camp manager not in contact with HQRM.

RESULTS AND RECOMMENDATIONS

- Expert advice has to be sought from current in-date professionals.
- The establishment of a multi-layered, variable option communications plan was based primarily on the paramount need for an effective safety net. Other communications considerations were secondary.
- The equipment chosen has to be handled and trained on by the whole of the team. We had our HF sets flown over from Canada so we could all get some hands on training and fault finding. Each team member had to be confident with the chosen equipment.
- A triple back-up procedure should be implicated for remote expeditions.

- Often Q&A sessions were held in the office by the team leader purposely directed at the Safety Emergency Plan. This bred a great deal of trust and confidence within the team.
- Once *in situ* a full safety plan mock procedure must be tested.
- Unless 100% confident in the equipment you have chosen, you must use a tried and tested piece, that has a history of success under the conditions you are going to encounter.

ADMINISTRATION PREPARATION & ENDORSEMENT

REQUIREMENT – GENERAL

Stage one

- Initial preliminary proposal to HQRM & DPNTS

Stage two

- Invitation to the Major Expeditions Committee (MEC)
- Present overall plan by PowerPoint to MEC
- Receive permission to plan further

Stage three

- Prepare initial finance plan
- Apply for service funding ASAP
- Source volunteers
- Team selection

Stage four

- Compose full expedition plan and deliver to HQRM & DNPTS
- Open expedition accounts
- Compile expedition brochure, letterhead paper and envelopes
- Design web page and post on the web ASAP
- Build team office and equipment
- Identify team responsibilities
- Inject the commando spirit and ethos into the trip

Stage five

- Devise full safety plan and deliver to MEC & HQRM
- Create final expedition plan and budget
- Team training promulgate team positions

- Develop the team
- Gain final diplomatic clearance

DIPLOMATIC – ROLE OF BRITISH DEFENCE LIAISON STAFF (BDLS)

BDLS Ottawa were initially informed at the earliest possible chance soon after the MEC approved further planning. The 'red tape' of any expedition must be addressed as soon as possible. This will help eliminate any future further snags. BDLS in our case were kept informed throughout the planning and preparation stages of the trip. BDLS will also help in the diplomatic clearance depending what country you intend to visit. BDLS with cultivation can be a very useful agency when applying for delicate diplomatic clearance.

ROYAL GEOGRAPHIC SOCIETY NOTIFICATION (RGS)

The RGS will undoubtedly add recognition and kudos to any expedition. The Society may endorse the trip depending on the extent of scientific exploration or pure exploration and adventure content. The endorsement of the RGS can be used as an advertising tool and also a lever for fundraising. Once returned from the venture they require a post-expedition report for the RGS archives to help others in their planning and preparation.

INSTITUTE OF NAVAL MEDICINE (INM)

We combined our training trips to Scotland, Iceland and Wales with the cold chamber at the Institute of Naval Medicine Gosport with a press facility organized by DPRN and SO1 PR HQRM. These proved excellent vehicles for building the interest and keeping the story topical in the news throughout our training phase. Team members contacted their hometowns and regularly conducted interviews with local tabloids and media. The INM provided the team with thermal photographs of their respective feet. The team also underwent thermal re-warming processes to determine cold spots on the feet.

'SPECIALIST' ENDORSEMENT

Depending on the severity and technical difficulty of the expedition, an outside agency endorsing your plan may be required. The Corps hosts many extremely talented explorers and adventurers; however, every topic may not be covered and there may not be a so-called 'expert' serving in the Corps.

We received our expert endorsement from one of the world's leading polar explorers, Dr David Hempleman-Adams. Not only did David endorse the trip but also he regularly invited us to his office to discuss the next stage of the planning phase.

David's influence and advice played a crucial part in the bonding and building of the team. He instilled confidence in our plans and further strengthened my belief in myself as a leader. Not only did David endorse the trip and our plan, he encouraged us to pursue a dream.

We gained great kind advice and experience from Pete Goss, who met the team on several occasions at Goss Challenges. He and his team provided support both materialistic and physiologically for the team. Guidance from Pete in many areas of project management and support for such a trip of this enormity was extremely beneficial for all. Since our return the team has delivered two separate presentations for audiences at Goss challenges, to add to the profile of TP2K a demonstration area showing the Royal Marines North Pole Expedition has been on show for several months.

PATRONAGE – MILITARY & CIVIL

To add weight to the trip within the Services, a suitable expedition patron should be requested to title the trip. We requested Admiral Sir Michael Boyce GCB OBE ADC and Major General RHG Fulton CGRM who graciously gave their support. A civilian patron could add valuable esteem to the expedition, especially if the majority of the fundraising had to be sought after commercially. If the expedition feels it needs Royal patronage, early application must be sent.

ADVENTURE TRAINING FORM (ATF) REQUEST 1

The ATF should be done ASAP with the help of IPT CTCRM and DNPTS. This will notify most of the normal adventure training departments of your proposed plan.

RESULTS & RECOMMENDATIONS

- More detailed requirements from the MEC should be available to the less experienced expedition leader.

- A major expedition template / guideline should be orchestrated for all large expeditions by the MEC.
- Heavily commercially funded expeditions will require the necessary vision and experience to appreciate fully the potential public relations and media interest the trip may generate. Such conditions must be integrated early into the expedition plan.
- The project officer must attend any high profile civilian meetings where the advertisement of the Corps is an issue.
- Early meetings with the Inspector of Physical Training at the CTCRM will help the leaders complete the ATF form and also contact the relevant funds at the earliest possible date.
- IPT CTCRM & unit PTI should hold the ATF form on computer disc. This would both enhance the presentation of the application and save time, which can be used for training. The ATF must be updated regularly and all key departments kept informed with the revised plan.

BASE CAMP ACTIVITIES

LOCATION

Resolute Bay Canadian NWT (Qausuittuq) Nunavut

OUTLINE DESCRIPTION

The base camp for TP2K was located at Resolute Bay on the southern shore of Cornwallis Island – 600km north of the Arctic Circle.

The hamlet of approximately 250 inhabitants is a unique blend of traditional Inuit and non-Inuit cultures. Three months without sunlight and temperatures to -50°C in the winter are balanced by 24-hour daylight throughout the summer months.

Located approximately 600km from the Magnetic North and 2000km from the Geographical North, Resolute Bay has been the base camp choice for many North Pole expeditions.

The people of Resolute are warm, friendly and welcoming. There are many services in this remote community, including three hotels and a co-operative store. Scheduled jet service is provided by a major airline plus a charter twin otter service to smaller communities. Several outfitters offer guided sport hunting opportunities, fishing trips, or Eco-tours and can supply you with equipment or logistical support if you choose to trek on your own.

The landscape that surrounds Resolute Bay and the wildlife that inhabits it are truly unique. Polar bear, arctic fox, musk ox and hare thrive in the high arctic and can be seen by visitors in almost any season. Resolute Bay is also one of the best locations to arrange a trip to observe high arctic wolves and the endangered Peary caribou. Pods of beluga and narwhal pass by Resolute Bay to summer feeding areas and can be viewed on boat tours or sometimes by simply walking along the beach.

The Resolute Bay area has attracted human settlement for the past 4,000 years. Near the present community lie the remains of four winter villages occupied by the early Inuit, who moved into the area from Alaska about 1,000 years ago. These sites include some of the earliest evidence of an Inuit presence in Arctic Canada. The people who lived here were efficient hunters of seal, walrus, beluga and bowhead whale. Their permanent winter houses were built from boulders and turf; whalebones support the roof.

Beechey Island, located 80 km east of Resolute Bay is the last resting-place for three members of the ill-fated Franklin Expedition. Franklin and his crew spent the winter of 1845-46 here, and many artefacts still remain today. Accessible by a short flight in a twin otter, visitors enjoy walking amongst the graves and pondering the mysteries surrounding this famous quest for the Northwest Passage.

Polar Bear Pass National Wildlife Area is located approximately 200km Northwest of Resolute Bay on Bathurst Island. Its primary purpose is to protect wetlands, which are critical nesting habitat for a variety of shorebirds, waterfowl, gulls, jaegers and snowy owls. In addition, the lush vegetation provides abundant food for mammals such as musk ox, caribou, as well as arctic foxes and lemmings.

The twin otter from Resolute Bay accesses Ellesmere National Park Reserve. During the brief arctic summer on Ellesmere Island, the sun remains high bathing the land in continuous daylight.

We left London Heathrow and after an overnight stay in Yellowknife, Canada, we arrived in Resolute Bay our final training destination and base camp. The initial details of the location and building were organized and finalized through the hamlet's Mayor. Once we settled in the proposed camp, the team were hampered by a lot of technical difficulties. This prompted the decision to leave the initial location and find alternative dwellings and facilities.

I thought we as a team were losing valuable training time trying to overcome problems that should have been sorted out prior to our arrival. As a leader, control and direction were needed, hence my decision to move to the South Camp Inn.

Once settled there with the IT equipment tested and operating satisfactorily, we were able to concentrate on final team selection and training. Once we had returned from the ice training, the base camp for the expedition was fully functional and tested. We were by then self-sufficient in stores and spare equipment, since prior to our arrival in Canada the RCAF had flown out all our bulk and heavy equipment to Resolute Bay with the base camp manager organizing the pick-up of our stores to the base camp .

This not only saved us time but considerable airfreight costs. The same method and transport route was chosen and executed once we had returned from the Pole. As a leader I had to have total confidence in the base camp and its facilities before venturing on the ice. The accountability of my team was paramount.

BASE CAMP TASKS TEAM POLAR 2000

- Monitor HF Radio.

In accordance with the Safety and Emergency Plan.

The radio schedules were carried out at either the base camp location or at First Air, located at the airhead. This proved to be a better set-up due to the position and elevation of the two radio masts.

- Monitor ARGOS.

The ARGOS proved to be an excellent asset to the expedition, lightweight, compact, and 100 percent reliable. This would send 95 positions to the Base camp every 24 hours.

- Send Situation Reports to our Rear Link UK via e-mail.

Up to two situation reports were sent back to the UK each week, until the final week when daily reports were returned. The website was updated using these reports.

- Log all emails, faxes, and ARGOS readings and press reports.
- Ensure re-supply kit prepared.
- Send updates and photos to adventure based websites, three adventure websites covered our expedition and made a link to our website:

www.adventure-mag.com

arcticculture.guide@about.com

www.expeditionnews.com

ASSISTANCE TO OTHER POLAR TEAMS

During our stay in Resolute we assisted other expeditions wherever possible.

Team Polar seemed to be in the minority by having their base camp located in Resolute. The Icelandic and Swedish team base camps were located in their home countries.

There are advantages and disadvantages in the choice of base camp locations; however, I think we were in a stronger position to react to any of the walker's requirements whilst they were out on the ice.

The following teams were assisted:

ICELANDIC TEAM: Loan of equipment, Photography.

EXEL LOGISTICS DAVE MILL: General help with admin, loan of equipment, filming and photography, Liaison with his PR company, return of freight to UK.

PAUL SHURKE – WINTERGREEN EXPEDITION: Daily Radio Schedules, e-mail situation report to his website, assist in planned re-supply.

LIAISON WITH FAMILIES AND NEXT OF KIN

Contact with families and next of kin was a high priority and we achieved this by regular phone calls and e-mail. We also arranged a basic phone patch so the Ice Party could talk direct to their family.

Updating families became more important due to some of the alarming press articles that appeared towards the end of the expedition and the mounting hardships the polar pair had to encounter in the latter stages of the trip. This aspect and particularly the morale effect of such links should not be underestimated.

MAGNETIC MEANDER

Dave Davenport, director of DXM LTD and the Jackson-Rowe Associates, three directors, joined us in Base camp for a weeklong Arctic experience. Dave and local guides ran this expedition and we helped with some general administration and local snowmobile touring and advice.

COMMUNITY RELATIONS

The aim during our stay in Resolute was to make a good impression on the community and we were successful in portraying the team and the Royal Marines in an exemplary light.

NON-EXPEDITION WORK

The hotel manager often asked for our help in various tasks around the hotel. This could range from taking his guests on snowmobile tours to standing in for the chef at breakfast! These small tasks helped the base camp to build a strong and good relationship with the community.

LEISURE TIME

The base camp party inevitably did have a great deal of free time, which was mainly spent touring the area on snowmobiles. In the evenings during the dark season, basketball, volleyball and five-a-side football matches were organized in the gymnasium, and one of the highlights in the hamlet is Bingo on a Friday night!

RESULTS & RECOMMENDATIONS

- It would have been better to send a daily update using the Argos reading from the beginning of the expedition so the web page could be updated more frequently. One of the common complaints we found regarding the website was the poor frequency of it being updated with new information.
- The base camp could have accessed the website to update it independently. This would have brought more real time reports to the expedition website. This would have had to have been arranged prior to the launch and the start of the walk.
- Funds should be earmarked for a recce of the base camp location.
- Military transport if available should be used to transport heavy items of equipment. This needs a lot of early warning, but reduces the cost immensely.
- In harsh remote areas, tried and tested equipment should be used. Trying to revolutionize the IT world under extreme conditions can jeopardize the whole plan and the lives of the team...
- The Ice Party, base camp and UK must enjoy three-way integrity at all times. This is crucial for decision-making by the leader and safety.

THE WALK

On March 8th 2000, four Royal Marines set off from Ward Hunt Island on what were to be the first steps into the world's polar history books.

TP2K, laden down with all the equipment and stores to last 60 days, started to walk north to the Geographical North Pole unsupported. This meant they would not receive any re-supplies, any airdrops, food caches, help from dog teams or computer satellite imagery. The still air temperature was -50°C.

Unsupported as opposed to supported throws a completely different policy on the expedition. The planning and research prior to the trip had to be meticulous and also very complex. Each item of equipment had to be able to provide a multitude of purposes. In conjunction to being multi-purpose the weight of each article had to be taken into account and kept to a minimum. Only one in 50 million people attempt to walk to the North Pole unsupported.

During the first week the team had to overcome pressure ridges thirty feet high and with razor sharp edges. Not only did we have to combat extreme physical challenges but also we had to survive and work in weather conditions exceeding temperatures of -50°C in still air. With only three hours of daylight to walk in at the start, the majority of all tent routines were conducted under candlelight and with the use of specialized head-torches.

Twice daily, medical checks were conducted and any ailments treated immediately. Every team member suffered from frost nip and mild frostbite, chafing between the legs and blisters on the feet. Royal Marines training and individual experience prevented anybody from being tormented with extreme cold weather injuries.

The expedition was broken down into seven manageable stages over the 472 nautical miles. The first three stages were completed early and without too much trauma. Our first encounter with trouble was when Charlie Paton fell and damaged his lower back at day 20. Soon after this incident he then fell through the ice up to his neck in freezing water at day 25. The drill practised by the team in base camp undoubtedly saved his life. Not only was he rescued immediately within three minutes; he was in a sleeping bag in fresh clothes drinking a hot energy drink. The Royal Marines' instinctive training and impulsive team drills ensured he survived.

The unfortunate discovery of Paul Jones' severe frostbite at day 30, meant he had to be evacuated from the ice as soon as possible to prevent further deterioration and possible gangrene infection. His decision to leave was a calculated, unselfish and definite one, founded on individual safety and team accountability. Coincidentally, Jason had been suffering from exhaustion and extreme internal pains for some time. His choice to join Paul on the evacuation plane three days later was a difficult but courageous and ultimately (as it turned out) sensible decision, since it transpired after hospital tests in the UK, that Jason Garland's body would not have been able to withstand any further physical exertion at such extreme temperatures.

After 30 relentless days on the pack ice, a non-emergency pick-up was orchestrated between the team leader and the SAR Company First Air in Resolute Bay. Two tents were erected and the injured pair waited in one tent for their evacuation. Charlie and myself lay in the second tent monitoring the radio waiting to speak to the incoming pilot. At no time did any of the TP2K base camp personnel fly on the rescue plane or have any contact with the Ice Party. The remaining pair on the ice had no contact physically with the plane apart from the HF radio. After three days Paul and Jason reluctantly and emotionally boarded the plane with all their supplies.

Once evacuated, the continuing pair re-distributed the remaining weight and pushed north, still unsupported, for what was to be a further 40 days.

The temperature had risen to a mild -30°C and we were now receiving 14 hours of daylight/twilight. The sledges were still quite heavy and we were now physically weak. A decision was made to discard some items of equipment. Once we had burned these items the sledges were lighter and our northerly progress increased daily. After 30 days' intense hard physical work we had burned off all our natural body fat and started to burn our way into muscle.

At this point, 25th April, we were now walking for 18 hours a day to try and catch up on lost time. Along the course of the day we would have to negotiate hundreds of semi-frozen leads and open stretches of icy water. Rafts were used by combining two sledges and also ski bridges were built to overcome these obstacles. Large open areas of water had to be walked around and it was one of these leads that nearly brought a halt to our progress. We had reached 89° north and we were running low on rations. We were held up by a three week white-out that made both of us snow-blind. After making emergency pinhole goggles from the card at the back of our diaries, we managed to keep crawling forward, frustrated by not being able to pick a decent route but driving forward.

We decided to head east around the open water, a decision that was to lead to success. After 15 hours of walking east southeast, we managed to gingerly cross the thinning ice. We were safely across; however, we were low on food, and had dropped the intake from 6,000 calories per day to 250.

This caused us extreme fatigue and hunger pains. From here we had 60 nautical miles left. A two day blizzard hampered our final approach and we were now ten days overdue and low on fuel. The food had finally finished three days previously and the polar pair was now walking 20 hours a day on tepid water.

Eventually, after 70 days man-hauling under the worst conditions in the world, TP2K reached the Geographical North Pole at 23:46 hrs on the 16th May 2000, the first British team to succeed unsupported from Canada. The ten week ordeal had taken its toll; Charlie and I had lost an incredible 45 pounds in weight each even though we consumed a total of 256,000 calories each.

EQUIPMENT MATTERS

The final selection of equipment and clothing for the expedition was the result of three years and extensive tests by myself. I spent six months in the previous winters testing and investigating every single item down to temperatures as low as -72°C.

After considerable time deciding between the team on the most modern clothing of the highest standard and durability, 18 months was spent writing to various companies for their sponsorship and support for our expedition. The positive return rate from civilian equipment and clothing outlets was 95%. A small but significant portion of the team's stores was produced from military sources, mainly the MCCW store in Coypool.

Due to the fact we chose to attempt to walk to the North Pole unsupported, weight and multi-purpose equipment were the two main influencing factors when the team were selecting the equipment. Each item had to do one if not more valuable jobs on the ice. If we decided that the item was not really needed or it was of a luxuriant nature, it soon became redundant and stayed in the UK. A few items were custom-made by the team in the UK and Resolute Bay. This was mainly to reduce the weight, which in turn made the items easier to use without removing our outer mittens.

Before the ice party departed for their start point, a full kit muster was conducted to ensure we had exactly all the correct items of the exact quantity and packed in their relevant locations. The average weight of each sledge was 244pounds of food, fuel and equipment. The majority of the weight was made up from rations and cooking fuel, which for an unsupported trip lasting 70 days was a sound achievement. Enough clothing and stores were produced to equip the base manager with sufficient attire for the duration of his stay in Resolute Bay, and out on the ice if the opportunity arose for a re-supply.

All the stores were secured into plastic sealed drums and freighted out to Canada six weeks prior to our arrival; with the help and support from the Royal Canadian Air Force it all arrived safely in Resolute Bay.

Once on the pack ice we experienced only a few minor failures, e.g. broken tent zips, sleeping bag zips and plastic sledge buckles. The main items of equipment and clothing proved to be excellent in all their properties and were of sound choice. Overall, the equipment, especially the clothing, withstood an extreme field test in a climate where you cannot afford to take second best, because survival and your life depends on its performance. We were extremely pleased with the selection of stores and equipment and would not change a great deal if we were to be in the same predicament and environment again.

PUBLIC RELATIONS

PLANNING

It was recognized early on that a trip of this magnitude would potentially gain significant global media interest. The task of going unsupported would also bring further attention, due to the severity of the expedition. We identified at an early stage that we needed a well thought out and controlled PR plan. The team put together a proposed plan and started to generate its own PR independently. Once we had gained national coverage from The Sun newsgroup, HQRM started to infiltrate the Royal Marines PR machine into the already progressing Team Polar PR plan.

To accompany the expedition we produced professional brochures, letterhead paper, compliment slips, business cards, a web page and a custom-made postcard to be posted from the top of the world (the latter promoted by The Sun). All of these helped raise the profile of the expedition and the Corps. The team wore a daily civilian expedition uniform and during physical training sessions long-sleeved tops were worn promoting the expedition with contact numbers and a web page address. The final piece of team promotion was the team mini-bus; this had the web page and the contact numbers designed on the sides and rear of the vehicle.

LAUNCH

To generate potential sponsors and further enhance the profile of the expedition, a launch was organized and orchestrated by Dave Davenport from

DXM Ltd. This would also act as an official start to the trip. Not only did the launch promote TP2K and the Corps, and it raised corporate funds for the trip by way of an auction. The launch was held in the Royal Air Force Club in London, and guests from both the business and military world were invited.

PRIOR TO THE DEPARTURE

Once the expedition had gained official recognition as a serious attempt at the Pole, the media interest started to grow. Numerous local interviews were conducted and a live PR facility was held in the expedition office. Seven separate television companies including a live satellite link up with Sky News recorded this. From there the team was self-sufficient in conducting press facilities and local reports either by phone, radio, or live link-up.

Once Johnnie Walker Whiskey joined as a financial sponsor, they brought the professional services of their PR agency. Red Consultancy, based in London, helped in organizing a string of interviews and PR opportunities prior to our departure. We were fortunate enough be able to access their network of potential PR contacts. The integration of DPRN, SO1 PR and Red Consultancy developed positively and was of significant value to the expedition.

THE WALK

Once in situ at the base camp all IT equipment and safety links were tested, not only as part of the safety plan but also to ensure the base camp had a direct link with all the sponsors, families and PR outlets.

The base camp received an update from the Ice Party; as described above this would be filtered down to the five key areas for immediate PR dissemination. These were DPRN, SO1PR HQRM, Red Consultancy, The Sun Newsgroup, and McKinney Rogers International. Once the press agencies had used the news it was then posted on the web page as an update. Many national and local papers ran a continuous story on the expedition for four months. This kept the trip alive in the public eye and helped in building the huge national interest as the Ice Party was closing on the Pole.

Once the Pole pair had reached the Pole and was ready for evacuation, a pre-planned 'end game' PR strategy was implemented. The co-ordination between DPRN, SO1 PR, Red Consultancy and independent television companies had to be fine-tuned. Unfortunately, the pilot who picked up the Ice Party from the

Pole could only stay on the ground for 20 minutes, which was not enough time to take all the footage planned or required. The expedition in its own right shot six hours of digital footage on route with a specially adapted camera and battery. To accompany the footage over 200 digital photographs were taken.

The expedition sacrificed the most up-to-date technology by means of computer and digital camera link, because of the weight. We had to achieve an idealistic weight to haul unsupported. Extra luxuries like the 'real time' camera were omitted.

POST EXPEDITION ACTIVITIES

Once back in the base camp we were initially planning to shower and de-service what equipment was left. This was not the case, the base camp had organized a full press facility. Four rooms were allocated for global interviews. We spent the next nine hours conducting endless, back-to-back press interviews. This was a great success and we managed to deliver the news real time across the world both through media and TV.

On our return, the team and Red Consultancy produced a CD-ROM with a 45 minute PowerPoint presentation, which was to be used as a launch for the TP2K lecture tour of both Service establishments and corporate companies. The presentation was given at the Royal Marines Museum initially, then to other interested parties. The full team only gave two talks, both self-organized. All other talks have been given individually or as part of a pair from the team at most.

The lecture tour, initially planned, never came to fruition. Privately, members of the team have delivered over 30 presentations, all organized by the team. Once the team disseminated after our return, just the team leader progressed further, delivering to the business world. However, whoever presents TP2K, will always come under the umbrella of the Royal Marines and we will continue to fly the Corps flag worldwide.

Some of the principal sponsors who backed the team are still using photographs and the facility of a speaker from the team to enhance and develop their product across the globe.

RESULTS & RECOMMENDATIONS

- Early coordination with HQRM and DPRN must take place to grasp the potential PR from major expeditions.

- Tight communications with the expedition's corporate financial sponsors.

- A strict PR aim should be followed throughout the expedition. This must be adhered to by all of the team and its immediate spokesperson.

- A precise but simple expedition brochure and letterhead paper should be used. 90 percent of begging sponsoring letters are unopened. The brochure and initial letter must be different and appealing to potential clients.

- A successful expedition showing great teamwork and leadership which incorporates the Corps ethos could be combined with a current UK DNR team. The expedition team could mirror the infrastructure of a DNR team, which has been already established and could deliver the TP2K presentation as an alternative side to the Royal Marines.

- Two-way communications between HQRM PR team and the team leader is vital. A constant, positive PR update must be published monthly and potential new avenues need to be maintained, nurtured and developed.

POST EXPEDITION ACTIVITIES -"CLOSEDOWN"

FUNDS

The expedition bank account was kept open to fund ongoing invoices from the post-expedition closing dinner and any outstanding bills from Canada. The expedition books were to be closed by the end of the final term 2000. Any outstanding monies would be returned to Corps funds for future expedition use.

LECTURES

The team will keep giving the TP2K presentation throughout the coming months, if not years. The presentation can be tailored for interest, leadership and team building purposes, depending on the audience. The team leader has delivered the majority of the post-expedition lectures, mainly to corporate companies.

TEAM OFFICE

Straight after the team disseminated from the team office and returned to their respective units, the office was returned back to the Education Centre at Norton Manor Camp. Not only was the office a working place, it also doubled as a secure building and storeroom for all the equipment.

TEAM DISSEMINATION

The team carried on working from the office at 40 Commando for a further three months after returning from Canada. The main tasks were to conclude the expedition in the way of equipment reports and returning of sponsor's equipment. Team members then returned to parent units with effect from August 2000. The team has never had the opportunity to meet up as a team since, due to unit commitments once disseminated.

REPORTS

Every equipment sponsor had a report written on the durability and performance of their individual item. To accompany the report, digital photographs were offered and used by their PR departments. The feedback from the expedition on all the equipment is a significant attraction for the manufacturer; a ten week field test for any item is priceless in the commercial world.

CONCLUSION

TP2K and the Royal Marines proved the impossible possible. The unsupported walk to the Geographic North Pole has always been the arctic grail, the unachievable. We brought success to ourselves, Great Britain and the Corps by well-managed, high performance teamwork. The training, planning and ability to listen to others helped in times of adversity and life and death decisions. Leadership is the loneliest job within a team; that's why it is so important to have the support, honesty and integrity of the whole team.

5 - Leadership Ethos

By Richard Hale

The success of the TP2K expedition and the achievements of Alan Chambers and the team attracted a great deal of interest at the highest levels. Indeed it was clear that Alan had also made a real impact in terms of his objective of raising the bar for leaders in all sectors and inspiring them to reach for ever challenging goals, to innovate and to leave a lasting legacy.

From the military sector there was congratulation from the highest levels of the British Army, the Royal Air Force and the Royal Marines. Letters of congratulation were received from very senior leaders in the British Forces.

It is interesting to note the pride shown on behalf of the Royal Marines and how Alan's leadership qualities are associated with the tradition of the Marine Spirit. At a technical level Alan had demonstrated the commando skills of survival and operating in extreme environments. However it is the personal qualities, as articulated by the commando spirit, which he is also recognized for. These qualities are defined as courage, determination, unselfishness, and cheerfulness in the face of adversity.

Most corporate organizations now have an expressed set of values and many have stated the key leadership capabilities they consider of importance. They try to develop these capabilities by linking them to performance management and assessment systems. It is may be instructive to compare the commando spirit qualities with your organization's stated values and leadership capabilities and competencies.

In corporate organizations there was a fashion in the 1980s and 1990s for experiential simulation-based team building exercises, often using the outdoors. In more recent years there has been a move away from this method of leadership development, or at least such development is under closer examination from the organizations investing in it, in order to challenge the value accrued. Katzenbach and Smith in their book *The Wisdom of Teams* advise against exercises which are fabricated to supposedly create a team. They say the best teams are formed through having a real purpose. For Alan Chambers and the TP2K expedition this purpose was defined in a very clear statement, 'to be the first British team to reach the Geographic North Pole from Canada unsupported.' The challenge was real, not a simulation and the activity and the learning was real; as Alan has said, 'It really happened.'

One might be misled into thinking that as a leader Alan adopted a stereotypical military style of leadership, relying on strict hierarchical command structures and an authoritarian style. However, this was not the case as he sought to involve all members of the team in decision making and gave all team members the opportunity to lead at different stages of the journey. His style of leadership may be seen as facilitative and very much aligned with the principles of future leadership outlined by the American action learning advocate and academic Joe Raelin. Raelin, drawing on research into the subject of leadership, proposes a new model of leadership for the future which is less about the leader as a hero and more about inclusion, involvement and action learning.

Future leaders will be 'linkers' who are skilled in recognizing and working with the strengths of different team members, who may have different work preferences. A good linking leader is a strong listener and able to coordinate activities across a range of types of work which have been identified as key to team performance. These include for instance:

Advising - providing information and professional advice

Innovating -the creation of and experimentation with ideas

Promoting - presenting and promoting services and products

Developing - introducing new systems, services and products

Organizing - organizing people and tasks

Producing -ensuring production and delivery of products and services

Inspecting - keeping control of procedures and systems

Maintaining - ensuring standards are maintained in care of products and people.

A leader who is strong in linking will demonstrate the skills shown below. It can be seen how Alan Chambers had to demonstrate these skills in setting up and then delivering on the TP2K expedition.

Alan made a point of listening to the views of all the team members, and 'tent time' was at the end of the day's walking, when team members would sit round in the tent and all have an opportunity to explain how they felt and to listen to each others' ideas on the way things are organized. Alan would also observe the levels of tiredness, comfort and make judgements as to when to intervene or allocate different tasks to individuals.

 Bringing people together for 'tent time' would ensure team members maintained open communication. Alan would encourage that any grievances about difficulties should be aired rather than suppressed. This would ultimately maintain good relationships, and he contrasts this with the 1998 expedition where he felt there were too many hidden agendas which did not become apparent until the team were on the ice, by which time it was too late.

A good linking leader also manages the interfaces between the team and external people and organizations which influence the success of the team. In the case of the TP2K expedition, this meant effective communication with base camp, but also knowing that whilst communications were severed, there was a high level of trust between the ice party and the base camp team. This was to prove critical at the point where the base camp asked the ice party if they were able to go on having been stranded on the ice flow. When Alan gave the response that they were 'focused but not blinkered' the base camp team knew that Alan wanted to continue and had done an effective risk assessment. The base camp team was trusted to communicate effectively with the outside world, including the press and sponsors.

If we look at the qualities identified as key to the commando ethos, these were also strongly displayed by Alan and they might equally be considered to as relevant leadership qualities for effective leadership in a business context. Quotations relating to the qualities of the commando spirit are taken from the Royal Navy website (http://www.royal-navy.mod.uk/).

Adaptability

"Is open to information and opinion from every available angle and able to adapt to this new knowledge. The Commando role demands an ability to adapt at short notice and to respond to new developments. An important principle during training is constant uncertainty, which breeds an ability to innovate and improvise and must be second nature to all members of the Royal Marines."

Humility

"The Royal Marines is an organization that is sometimes criticized for its understated approach. This is not just false modesty; arrogant organizations believe they have little to learn from others, and arrogance leads to inflexibility and rigidity. In order to adapt and innovate it is essential that the Corps, while proud of its standards, remains sufficiently self critical – humble enough – to recognize and adopt the good practices of other institutions. Humility also contributes to the essential bond between all ranks and on operations allows us to work with considerable success."

Professional Standards

"The three group values so far are shared by many other non-military institutions; it is these, coupled with an adherence to the highest professional standards as amphibious commandos that

ensures the success of the Royal Marines as a military force. The environment in which commandos operate is complex, dangerous and uncertain, and successful action in this sphere requires the highest professional standards."

Fortitude

"It is fortitude that underpins achievement rather than simply physical fitness. Whilst fitness remains a critical component of our success, it will not, by itself, guarantee it…individual and collective fortitude; mental will that builds upon, but goes beyond, professional skills and physical fitness."

Alan has a personal vision of wanting to create and leave a legacy. This is about raising the profile of leadership nationally and internationally. By telling his story to thousands of business leaders each year, and by taking many leaders on trips to the North Pole he encourages leaders to consider their own purpose and the legacy they want to leave. Considering the legacy you want to leave is a profound question and to some it may sound ephemeral and difficult to define. However, if you are able to answer this question, or at least to give it serious consideration, then this should inform your actions and behaviours as a leader.

American advocate of action learning, Joe Raelin, who is based at Northeastern University, Boston proposes a very relevant new model of leadership in his article *'Does Action Learning Promote Collaborative Leadership'*. He proposes a collaborative approach to leadership based on the humanistic principle; that if people are involved in a participative way in their organization or project, they will be committed. He sees future leadership as about introducing the concept of mutual inquiry and a non-judgemental approach, encouraging people to put their ideas forward so that new ideas might surface. He says leadership has these qualities:

Concurrent: there can be more than one leader operating in an organization, power is shared and overall is increased through the sharing. Different leaders emerge at different times for different tasks

Collective: it is a plural phenomenon, the process of leadership derives from people working together and anyone may arise to serve the group's leadership needs. There may be a formal leader but this is not always the most important leadership role. Team members learn and make meaning together.

Mutual: all members are in control and may speak for the entire organization or project, people are assertive but also sensitive and listening, open about beliefs with others, every opinion is genuinely considered.

Compassionate: leaders extend unconditional commitment to preserving the dignity of others and stakeholders are considered before making a decision without worrying about status. The leader is adaptable and encourages democratic participation.

It is interesting to consider the convergence in terms of the leadership thinking across Alan Chambers' approach in leading the TP2K expedition, the academic and corporate view of future leadership and the qualities embodied in the commando spirit.

Alan Chambers comments on his observations of some of the business leaders he has observed on his North Pole trips:

'I have seen a lot of leaders who lead by fear. Some leaders who can hold the future of the organization and thousands of people in their hands. Their people are scared to speak out and fear for their livelihood. I have seen some changes and I have met some extremely influential leaders who put the boundaries down and then open up to their teams, inviting them to generate ideas for the business as to how things can be improved.'

Alan believes there is value in taking leaders out of their normal business environment in order to bring out some of their real qualities and this emerges from these trips where they are working, living and surviving together on the ice:

'It is an emotional challenge, it is a testing environment, and some of the people have never previously slept in a tent, let alone worked in -25°C. But it is all about choices, people have to make decisions and choices when they train for six months. They have to choose on a Sunday do they train or do they go and play golf with their mates. We never tell anybody they have to do it. It is about personal choice: they have to prepare themselves so they don't let themselves or the team down. A lot of the training they do and commitment happens from a distance, they have to take a deep personal commitment – they have to change how they operate. We are taking them deeper. It is so easy to say 'there is no way I could achieve this.' These people are most frightened of failure. Here we are putting them in an environment where they don't know how they are going to perform in front of a peer group. It is getting people to accept they have got more inside them. They have a lot more inside them. It is courageous of them doing something they have never done before. They have to ask themselves the question about how are they perceived and will this add value to how they are perceived. The North Pole is not a given. It freezes and melts every year. The people are different, the terrain is different. We know what the long term goal is but they have to make daily and hourly decisions and consider how they are going to influence people to get through the next hour. Often the biggest learning points they gain is coming from the tree tops to the roots. For them all there is a major emotional impact. They don't have the trappings of leadership around them. It would be easy to work out a hierarchy, who has set up the biggest company or who is the wealthiest, but in this environment everyone has to be treated equally. I have every respect for what these people have achieved in their business life, but on the ice they have to be judged based on what they do on the ice during the day.'

One of the qualities described as important in the ethos of the Royal Marine commandos is the ability to tell stories. These provide key messages concerning the history, the folklore and the values of the organization which are reinforced by word of mouth. This has been institutionalized and is encouraged. In corporate organizations it is often through storytelling that similar outcomes are achieved. Alan Chambers' story, of the 'successful failure' and the 'ultimate success' have also inspired many leaders and teams from quite different organizations.

In the field of sport the stories have proven an inspiration at critical periods of challenge. For instance, Alan spoke to the England cricket team before they went into the 2005 Ashes competition with Australia. The Ashes is a series of matches associated with fierce rivalry dating back to 1882 and England won the 2005 series, their first win since 1985. This was a series of highs and lows with a nailbiting finish and will go down in history as one of the most exciting ever. Duncan Fletcher the England coach recounts his experience of the impact of Alan's story, upon what was ultimately to become an historic series victory for England. Here is Duncan Fletcher OBE in his own words from the book *Ashes Regained – The Coach's Story*, explaining the contribution of Alan's input before the first test match at Lord's had:

'… what a remarkable man, and what a remarkable story he had to tell us. For in 2000 he and fellow Royal Marine commando Charlie Paton became the first Britons to reach the geographical North Pole without support, dragging their 250lb sledges 500 miles across the ice from Canada. Their party had begun as four but two others pulled out, one through exhaustion and the other through frostbite, as Chambers and Paton survived temperatures as low as -30 degrees C on as little as half a cup of porridge a day. The day before they reached the Pole and raised the Union flag on the top of the world, they ran out of food.

Chambers was subsequently awarded the MBE for his determination and strong leadership in the worst polar weather for 20 years…It was some story. It could easily be said we lost the Test after we heard it, and that it had no effect. But it did have an effect. Long into the Test series, there were still calls of 'Remember the Iceman' being heard in the dressing room. He told us one story of how they were on an iceberg which was drifting away from the main ice tract and of their battle to get back on track. We used that analogy after we lost this Test at Lord's.'

Fletcher goes on to recount how Alan kept in touch throughout the series at each twist and turn, recounting parallels with his journey and these messages of support proved highly motivational.

Mathew Hoggard MBE, a key team member, also gives due credit to Alan for inspiring the team with his story:

'A couple of days before the Lord's test, we had a motivational speech from Alan Chambers, the explorer... He told us about some days on their expedition when they had managed to walk a mile forwards, but the ice had shifted backwards two miles, so they found themselves a mile farther back than they had started. The determination those blokes showed was pretty inspiring.'

(The Times, 14th September, 2005)

Michael Vaughan OBE, the England captain, said:

'…Before the Test we had the explorer Alan Chambers give us a presentation on how he got through a walk to the North Pole - an amazing journey of endurance, skill and strength. There were parallels to be shared and he told us there would be blips and setbacks along our route. After the first test I remembered what he said....'

Interestingly after England went on to lose the Ashes tournament in 2006 with a 5-0 whitewash many critics were quick to lampoon the coach Duncan Fletcher, but what was to follow in January and February 2007 with the one day series was remarkable and due credit was given to the influence of Alan Chambers. England were to show incredible resilience in the face of adversity and bad press, as they bounced back to win the Commonwealth one day series. The words of David Hopps reporting in The Guardian are quoted below:

'England's tour of Australia ended in surreal fashion, with a browbeaten side recovering their vigour to win the Commonwealth one-day series and Duncan

Fletcher extolling the words of Mother Teresa as his inspiration during the bleakest period of the Ashes winter. "Mother Teresa said that when you are successful you win some unfaithful friends and some genuine enemies".

'Mother Teresa' comment was given to Fletcher by Alan Chambers, a motivational speaker and polar adventurer, who first spoke to England before their successful Ashes campaign in 2005. Chambers led the first British team to walk unsupported to the North Pole. England's coach has got through with the help of a man who won the MBE for "determined leadership in constant adversity" and a religious worker known as "the saint of the gutters". Well as everyone knows it has been a tough tour.... "We call Alan Chambers the Ice Man", Fletcher said. "We use him to psychologically boost the side up. Spoke before the Ashes. He has kept in touch with me. It was all about an endurance test. He has sent me a few e-mails during this tour. He has been the most positive individual who has spoken to me on the tour."

The parallels with Alan having to demonstrate the resilience to bounce back from the 'successful failure' of the 1998 attempt on the North Pole to success in 2000 are plain to see.

Additionally, in Rugby Union, Alan inspired the England team before they won the 2003 World Cup. Martin Johnson OBE, the captain of the team said:

'...Alan's amazing story, highlighting the remarkable focus and leadership he had around the North Pole trip, truly inspired the team in their preparation for the Rugby World Cup...'

We hear below from leaders in the business environment who have joined Alan on his trips to the North Pole and it is clear to see the value, which they gain from the experience. These trips are by no means tourist trips. They are designed to enable industry leaders to work out their personal leadership questions and through the experience of walking around fifty miles to the North Pole. The trips provide a radically different context for leaders to work through their understanding of leadership and of themselves as leaders. Here we provide in their own words the accounts of leaders who have done this.

Richard Eyre

Richard Eyre has pursued a most successful career in the media sector, which includes roles as Chief Executive Officer of Capital Radio, Chief Executive Officer of the ITV Network, Chairman and Chief Executive of Pearson Television and Chairman of RDF Media. He is also Chairman of the Interactive Advertising Bureau and a director of The Eden Project in Cornwall, UK.

What was your purpose in going on the North Pole trip....?

I was 50 years old a few days after we returned. So in some ways, the decision to go to the Pole was a gesture of defiance, a challenge to myself to push past familiar boundaries and do something big. But the factor above all else that made me sign up was Alan's statement that *'You cannot go to the North Pole and come back unchanged'*. These words bugged me. I couldn't imagine what could be so big that it would to change a person whose assumptions and understanding of life were pretty well worked out.

My objectives were accomplished and I now know what Alan's promise meant.

What were the biggest challenges for you personally?

The relentlessness of the process. Even going to bed was not relaxing, squeezing your feet into a sleeping bag that had been frozen into a ball. When it got warm it merely got damp. So the night was as much of a challenge as the day.

How has the experience helped you as a person/as a leader?

I think we all have an instinct that whatever lies beyond the familiar is dangerous - best not to venture there. The North Pole trip was proof that you don't know until you go there.

How does any of your experience or learning translate back into the business or work context?

It does absolutely. This is especially so in the area of risk. The failure to embrace risk radically reduces financial and other types of profit. Alan stated that we were not avoiding risk; we were embracing it, but only after understanding it. This is a highly important point for leadership in business.

What did you experience in terms of leadership during the trip – either from yourself, or other participants?

Leadership is service. Alan, Charlie and Ann worked harder than all the rest of us, pulling bigger weights, walking alone till they found ways across the leads as well as managing communications, repairs and supervision of the trip. They each earned our respect in a way that any alternative approach would not have achieved.

How can others learn from your experience?

I hope I have become a better leader. I think many of us live our lives within boundaries defined by our confidence, our experience or role models. If I can challenge people to contest their assumptions about what they can achieve, as the North Pole did for me, this would be success indeed.

What do you see as the key qualities of an effective leader?

You must be capable of earning respect. In the end, you're only a leader if someone trusts you enough to follow.

What is the legacy you would like to leave as a leader?

To be an inspiration.

Alison Levine

Alison was born with a life-threatening heart condition that precluded most demanding physical activities. Surgery has changed her life and she has pursued a remarkable career. She has had corporate leadership roles in healthcare, technology and finance including working on Wall Street with Goldman Sachs. In 2003, she left Wall Street to serve as Deputy Finance Director for Arnold Schwarzenegger in his successful bid to become Governor of California. She was once named one of San Francisco's Top Business Leaders Under 40. As an adventurer and climber she was team captain of the first American Women's Everest Expedition. She is founder of Daredevil Strategies™ and Climb High Foundation, a non-profit organization that trains jobless women in Africa to be mountain guides.

What was your purpose in going on the North Pole trip?

I went on the trip because the North Pole seemed like the ultimate challenge. A totally barren, harsh environment place where you only have yourself and your team to rely upon. I've been to harsh environments before having climbed mountains all over the world, but there are generally other people around. This time it was going to be ALL US. I knew the team dynamics would be both challenging and fascinating. I had also never cross-country skied, and I thought this was about as good a place to learn as any.

To what extent did you feel you achieved your objectives?

I observed some of the most amazing displays of teamwork I had ever seen. There was no sense of competition - everyone really joined forces to help everyone else during the tough times and the easy times. When someone gets an injury on a mountain or wants to quit, they can turn around and go home. That was not the case here, and everyone supported each other physically and mentally.

What were the biggest challenges for you personally?

Trying to understand the different accents! I couldn't understand a lot of people, and I felt like a bonehead asking people to repeat themselves all the time. The other challenge for me was just learning how to cross country ski on that type of terrain. I was thinking it was going to be flat - but the pressure ridges really get you.

How has the experience helped you as a person/ as a leader?

It helped me understand that sometimes you can't move in the direction you want to go in when you are working toward a goal. It has helped me have patience by realizing that sometimes you have to take the whole team and go for miles in what you think might be the wrong direction in order to get to your final destination, and you can't get discouraged along the way.

How does any of your experience or learning translate back into the business/work context?

Oh, there is a direct correlation as I am reminded that everything will always be in constant motion, and the horizon might look one way at one moment and then might change very quickly to look completely different. And sometimes you like what you see and sometimes you don't, but you still have to keep moving toward your goal.

What did you experience in terms of leadership during the trip - either from yourself, other participants.

The thing that really stuck with me about the trip was observing people who were what I call *'silent leaders.'* I watched people step up to the plate and play roles as leaders without beating their chests and wanting attention or credit. I observed people taking on extra physical burdens during the process of helping others not because they thought they'd be admired for it, but because they truly cared about their team-mates. It was magical. You don't always get group dynamics like that. It's very, very rare.

What have you taken from the adventure in terms of learning about leadership?

People's true abilities can always be tested in extreme environments. You really learn what you're made of and you learn what the people around you are capable of, or are incapable of as well.

How can others learn from your experience?

I hope others will understand the importance of getting off the couch and getting out of their comfort zone.

What do you see as the key qualities of an effective leader?

Someone who empowers others to think like leaders as well. Someone who doesn't let fear stop them from doing what they think is the right thing to do. Someone who is not afraid to take responsibility for both people and circumstances, whether he or she has control over them or not.

What is the legacy you would like to leave as a leader?

That you can be a strong leader and still be kind, caring and loving.

Kevin D Gaskell

Kevin D Gaskell is former Managing Director of Porsche Cars Great Britain Limited and BMW GB Limited. Currently CEO of Eurotax Glass International SA.

What was your purpose in going on the North Pole trip?

To join a team who were setting out to achieve something pretty special and to embrace and enjoy the challenge which that offered…and, along the way to collect a meaningful amount of sponsorship for cancer research.

To what extent did you feel you achieved your objectives?

Objectives fully achieved. In the space of only a couple of weeks I became part of a team that will share a close bond for a very long time, understood the challenge of facing an extremely hostile environment and raised enough money to build a new cancer unit.

What were the biggest challenges for you personally?

Getting fit enough to do the trip – not easy when you live the life of an international executive hobo. Understanding the savage environment in which we were operating, realising that we were fully responsible for our safety and that of the members of the team around us.

How has the experience helped you as a person / as a leader?

It has made me realise more than ever the value of planning and preparation. It has led me to have more confidence and trust in those specialists who know more about a given environment or situation than I do. It has improved my patience realising that we need every member of the team to complete the course and that most of us, including and especially me, will need assistance at some point.

How does any of your experience or learning translate back into the business / work context?

I lead multi national teams and now appreciate more fully that precise communication and understanding of role and responsibilities is the key to the successful achievement of objectives. Operating in a hostile environment demonstrated this very clearly as you only wish to do tasks once.

What did you experience in terms of leadership during the trip - either from yourself, or other participants.

That everyone in a team is a leader given the opportunity and support. That leadership takes many forms including, for example, being a positive and encouraging team member – an action which in itself will enhance the overall dynamics, motivation and success of the team. That leadership does not always mean being the guy out front, that it may be the guy helping the slower walkers at the back, or the girl doing everything the guys do with a smile and a positive word for all.

What have you taken from adventure in terms of learning about leadership?

That as a leader my role is to set objectives clearly, communicate the goals effectively and then encourage others to accept responsibility for delivery of the project. That team members who are positive motivation leaders are leaders in their own right and are a vital element of the team's success. That you have to trust and support the specialists and not second guess. That leaders need to support, support and support again the team's progress.

How can others learn from your experience?

They can already see that I am a calmer, more considered leader. I try to apply the lessons learned from this experience to my role as an international CEO and build teams who understand and share a clear vision of success – and then encourage and motivate them to achieve their goals. When events go off track I don't seize back responsibility to resolve the issue but rather encourage and empower the team to resolve the issues and to be successful.

What do you see as the key qualities of an effective leader?

Someone who has the ability to visualise success and who can then clearly share that vision with the individuals in the team in a way that motivates and empowers the team to achieve the goals. Someone who enables and encourages the team to take the credit for their own success.

What is the legacy you would like to leave as a leader?

That when I am gone the successful team believes they did it themselves…

Simon Virgo

Managing Director, 1st Scaffolding

What was your purpose in going on the North Pole trip?

My purpose for going on the trip to was to test myself in difficult conditions, have a great time and to reach the pole. Fundamentally this trip was about a group of people combining their own sets of skills and characteristics to reach the objective. In that vein, we were all there to see how well we could apply our business team skills into a very adverse and challenging environment.

To what extent did you feel you achieved your objectives?

Number one, we made it to the Pole. Overall however I think I learnt a lot about my own ability to confront challenges head-on. The trip also made me want to go a little further and try to make extra contribution to get us all there. And we certainly had a great time - well, I know I did!!

What were the biggest challenges for you personally?

Physically I was prepared although the arctic environment will always present a challenge in itself. For me, the hardest part was handling the variety of personalities and the different ways such a diverse group dealt with the difficulties. But this was where I learnt the most about myself.

How has the experience helped you as a person/as a leader?

As a person the experience and memories of the trip will live with me for a long time - I'll be dining out on it for years! As a leader, it has given me greater strength to deal with some of the harder aspects of managing people.

How does any of your experience or learning translate back into the business/work context?

The biggest aspect of learning relates to dealing with the way that different people deal with adversity. After years of smaller expeditions and of business leading, this really surprised me and has made me re-think the way I treat people.

What did you experience in terms of leadership during the trip - either from yourself, or other participants?

I saw excellent leadership in terms of the three expedition leaders, albeit in 3 unique styles. I also saw what happens when you put a group of people who lead for a living into the mix. Contributions in this vein were high until we moved out of our comfort zones and then we saw everybody at their best, or at least kind of! I think we all know what we're good at now!

What have you taken from adventure in terms of learning about leadership?

It's evident that leadership cannot be learnt easily but its also striking that leadership can be learnt more effectively in adverse mental and physical conditions. If the opportunity came up I'd take my entire sales and operations team up to the Arctic for a long walk...

How can others learn from your experience?

Of course, our friends learn from our constant droning on about the trip! More importantly I think the trip has broadened my horizons and my self-awareness and that can only be good for family and friends.

What do you see as the key qualities of an effective leader?

Decisiveness, humour, risk management, self-awareness, integrity, communication, selflessness, the ability to motivate others.

Angelo Speranza

CEO Burlodge Ltd

What was your purpose in going on the North Pole trip?

I have been fascinated by the Artic and its harsh environment since a young age and dreamt that one day I would experience it. I also wanted to experience being in an alien environment which completely removes you from the modern ways of living.

To what extent did you feel you achieved your objectives?

I achieved my objectives to the full and to my surprise the most enjoyable part of the trip was the interaction and the closeness of the team followed by the scenery and environment we were in.

What were the biggest challenges for you personally?

Making the decision to go and the not knowing the other team members and how I would get on with them.

How has the experience helped you as a person/as a leader?

It has made me appreciate that experiences outside the working environment are important too. The planning and dedication required to prepare for any undertaking is crucial to a successful outcome and that the most difficult step in any undertaking is not finishing but starting.

How does any of your experience or learning translate back into the business/work context?

Once you have started be prepared for changing course to achieve your goal and be flexible in these course changes even if it deviates from your original plan, what is important once you have started is getting there. You are part of a team and you are as strong as your weakest member, so be prepared to help when someone needs it and do not fear asking when you need help.

What did you experience in terms of leadership during the trip either from yourself, or other participants?

What has struck me the most on this trip in terms of leadership is that we can all be leaders to a certain degree in the areas we are comfortable with but bad leaders in areas they are not. Good leaders usually have a good understanding of the situation they are in and make decisions accordingly but they also need to be comfortable in the environment they're in.

What have you taken from adventure in terms of learning about leadership?

Brief your team all the time, give them short term objectives and remind them of the ultimate goal. Leaders should always show that they are under control also when they are not. Do not be afraid to ask for advice or opinion from your team and make them part of decision making. Be firm when you need to be.

How can others learn from your experience?

From a personal point of view I hope to have shown others that everything is possible and that once one gets going, the rest will fall into place. From an environmental point of view we need to make big changes in the way we live to limit the environmental impact.

What do you see as the key qualities of an effective leader?

A good thinker and motivator, a team player, a person who sets clear objective and plans, one who accomplishes its objective and plans, a person that talks the talks and walks the walk, a person that has the esteem and respect of his team, an honest and generous person.

What is the legacy you would like to leave as a leader?

None, as I hope my successor is all the above points and better than I am and will lead to even better things.

David Stob-Stobbart

Former investment banker

What was your purpose in going on the North Pole trip?

I guess the answer's in 2 parts: when first learning about it, and then when coming to grips with what was involved. The first was more about being in such a 'cool' place and also being perceived by friends and family as doing something challenging and different. Then, as the logistics and fundraising kicked in, more and more people asked me 'why?'. On bad days the reply was a curt 'Why not ...'. It's easier with the benefit of hindsight to now articulate it better. I was after something to focus on beyond the day-to-day grind; something where I was the primary beneficiary; something where I could feel good about helping the Charity; something to challenge me into places I never thought I would go; something where I could learn from people I wouldn't normally come into contact with.

To what extent did you feel you achieved your objectives?

There were four practical objectives: to reach the Pole, comfortably; to get fitter in the training; to make a film of the expedition; to raise a certain target of money. All four were met.

There were two personal objectives: to learn about managing and leading a team into this sort of environment; and to see how I coped in adverse situations where I was tested physically.

The first was met: It was a great team of people with such diverse backgrounds. The leaders (Phil, Alan, Pete, Anne, Charlie) had very different styles and each played vital leadership roles at various stages. Flexibility of style is a hard lesson to learn, but a crucial skill to have!

The second personal objective (coping) wasn't fully met. It never got as cold as I had hoped, and I was sad to finish (can't we walk back as well?). While completely enjoyable – I wasn't pushed enough physically. I guess that leaves a bit over for the next trip!

What were the biggest challenges for you personally?

At the time, there were only a few niggles, like waking up to bad breakfast with a smile (I don't do mornings); I had some minor issues filming on a few of the days on account of the weather (funny that); the usual lack of space in the tents (especially when you're the pedantic type).

But looking back, I'd have to say patience. Patience for the slower teams. Patience for the crossing of leads like a pack of kids on a school outing. Patience for the weather. Patience for the lack of progress. I know I wasn't the only one to suffer this. The easy answer was to take my mind off it by focusing on the filming!

How has the experience helped you as a person/ as a leader?

It's been fantastic at dinner parties. But on a slightly deeper note, it's woken me up to other possibilities and how little fun I was having before. It gave me the courage to change direction in my professional life and try something new. It's given me a fantastic milestone which I use regularly to look back and evaluate how I'm doing. I recommend it to everyone.

How does any of your experience or learning translate back into the business/work context?

I think I can appreciate and recognize the same sort of feelings in other people much better now. Going back to an earlier point about style: I'm much more aware of being able to adapt to situations and try and use different styles. Can't say I'm an expert but I do get reminded about its importance regularly.

What did you experience in terms of leadership during the trip - either from yourself, other participants?

The team was made up of some truly distinguished leaders in their own fields. It brought home – perhaps today more than in the past – how difficult it is to be the dominant leader all the time. In fact, this sort of attitude to leadership would have been undesirable and riddled with conflict. In a team of equals - coping with the day to day - leadership became more about taking responsibility for your work, communicating well, being attentive to those around you, helping out when needed. A role that everyone can and must play.

Of course, there were times when critical decisions have to be made. Perhaps quickly. That's when it helps to have trust in those more experienced than you as well as clear roles and responsibilities.

So adapting to the situation is critical.

What have you taken from adventure in terms of learning about leadership?

Everything. I find in big business that all too often the game is politics and committees. Adventure is much more fun and much more immediate! It's a much faster and better classroom to learn about yourself, other people, managing and leading. You may even get to fail occasionally and learn something without being fired. And what's more – you don't have to use flipcharts, ring binders and back copies of the Harvard Business Review!

How can others learn from your experience?

Read the books so that you get to learn the language and how to think and talk about things. Then get out and just do it.

What do you see as the key qualities of an effective leader?

Experience

Rapport

Communicates well (listens more often than speaks)

Propensity to act (and how this is conducted)

Sense of humour (with a sprinkling of humility)

Emotional stability (with a dollop of passion)

What is the legacy you would like to leave as a leader?

Don't think I know the answer yet. I'd like to have tried something big and hopefully succeeded at it. I'd like the journey to have been interesting. I'd like to have done it with people I enjoy being around, who regularly teach me things but also don't mind being taught occasionally. I'd like to inspire someone else to do something they considered too big before they started.

Chris Heminway

Industrial Advisors LLP

What was your purpose in going on the North Pole trip?

Having led a relatively desk-bound existence for the last 20 years, the opportunity to do something more physically challenging yet within the bounds of what I thought would be realistically achievable was what sold me on the idea of a trek to the Pole.

To what extent did you feel you achieved your objectives?

My objective was to get to the North Pole no matter what was thrown at us in the way of challenges along the way. That the majority of the group successfully made it despite the problems of poor ice and significant drift in the first few days meant that my objectives were achieved.

What were the biggest challenges for you personally?

Personally speaking, the biggest challenge was dealing with camp life at the end of each day and the start of the next. Squatting in cramped conditions for hours on end in order to melt sufficient ice for food re-hydration and drink is, I suspect for most men, a physically uncomfortable experience and, personally, more demanding than walking a 12-hour day.

How has the experience helped you as a person/as a leader?

The trek brought home to me that the limitations of a team of people who are striving to achieve a common goal is defined by the weaker rather than stronger members of the team. The work that we put in together to ensure that everyone that was able to make it did so was a refreshing and rewarding experience.

How does any of your experience or learning translate back into the business/work context?

The trip was also a stark reminder that, in any aspect of life but particularly in business, you have to know your own limitations and rely on the help and assistance of others more qualified than you when necessary

What did you experience in terms of leadership during the trip - either from yourself, other participants.

Every team has to have its leader, which must be someone in whom you place your trust to make the right decisions. While the dangers we faced when on the ice were not immediately life-threatening in themselves, placing your safety in the hands of someone else requires a leader deserving of that confidence – which I would categorically state that we had in Alan.

How can others learn from your experience?

I would recommend that anyone that wishes to understand how a team of people need to work together should take on a trek like the North Pole Challenge

What is the legacy you would like to leave as a leader?

As someone who has lead people in a business environment, I'd like to think that a leader should inspire by example but also teach the principles of respect to and for each and every member of a team.

6 - Action Based Leadership Development in Business

by Richard Hale

In this chapter Richard Hale discusses his views on executive leadership development and learning in the corporate world. These views and proposals have been formed through a combination of learning from his own experience over a period of 25 years of working in the field of management and leadership development with organizations in a number of business sectors ranging from major financial institutions to technology and fast moving consumer goods. This has led to his view that executive leadership development should be focused on learning from action and real leadership problems. This thinking can be related to the experiences of Alan Chambers who, as seen in the previous chapters, has been recognized for outstanding leadership through a mind-set which is constantly hungry for learning and innovation; he also realizes the importance of focused research and learning 'with and from others' which is an essential tenet of action learning.

How Should We Measure Learning?

It is over 45 years since Donald Kirkpatrick published a model for the evaluation of training suggesting it should take place at four levels. These levels were:

1. Reactions – are people happy with the training inputs?

2. Learning – what do people remember from the training sessions?

3. Behaviour – do people use what they know at work?

4. Work Results – the outcomes of applications on the job over a period of time?

Since the publication of the original model we have witnessed dramatic change in organizational structures, cultures, technologies and training methods. Yet the HR, training and development community continues to rely predominantly on the old Kirkpatrick model in discussing the evaluation of training.

It has, however, proven a model that is difficult to use for evaluation of learning at all four levels in practice. In a USA-based survey, only 7 percent of organizations surveyed evaluated the return on investment in training. In the UK, 57 percent of organizations surveyed said evaluation was becoming more important, but only 27 percent were using action plans after training.

The time has come to reformulate how we view evaluate training and this relates particularly to the training and development of leaders. The example set by Alan Chambers in demonstrating not just exceptional leadership through his expeditions, but an exceptional approach to his personal learning is one we can draw on for inspiration. In one sense he demonstrates the obvious; that learning takes place through action.

I would like to expose some of the myths around training and development and present some new approaches to assessing effectiveness. This has evolved from experience with new models of training design applied in major international organizations. These cases show the benefits of placing the responsibility for evaluation firmly on the shoulders of the learners. Also we can see that true learning is inextricable from action and the work environment.

Research by the American Society for Training and Development has provided the following picture of how companies actually approach evaluation of training at each of the levels suggested by Kirkpatrick.

Percentage of companies that use each level of post-training evaluation	
Level 1 (reaction)	78%
Level 2 (testing for learning)	32%
Level 3 (behaviour change)	9%
Level 4 (ROI)	7%
Source: American Society for Training and Development 2002 State of the Industry Report	

Kirkpatrick (1996) in a more recent summary of his original work, proclaimed that evaluation should be used to help training directors sell more training. He says:

'The future of training directors and programs depends to a large extent on their effectiveness. To determine effectiveness attempts should be made to measure training in scientific and statistical terms.'

There is a lot in this comment. I would agree with the first sentence but I do not see the solution as straightforward as that expressed in the second. I believe there a number of myths about executive training and development that have developed in the latter part of the 20th century which we now need to expose and challenge. Training and executive development specialists have become locked into the Kirkpatrick conceptual framework and this quest to become 'scientific' and 'statistical'. I realize this has often been because of a desire to prove their own worth professionally, but it has often led to attempts to apply pseudo-scientific and statistical methods to the measurement of the effectiveness of development interventions, whereas actually a different approach may provide more value. Here are some of the myths which have arisen.

Myth No. 1 - Learning is the Responsibility of the Trainer

Training evaluation should serve to protect the role of the training professional. Many HR and training professionals have indeed worked to this protectionist model, with the prime purpose of their evaluation efforts being to justify their position. Line managers and recipients of executive development have been happy to go along with this. After all it takes the heat off the learner or business leader if he or she can throw the onus for evaluation back onto the trainer, the HR function or the consultant delivering the training. If they cannot prove the value of the training, and invariably they can't, then it is down to the provider to 'try harder', not the learner.

Such thinking works against the espoused principles of ensuring learners take responsibility for their own learning. If you are to take responsibility for your own learning that should not only include contributing to the identification of your needs and possible solutions, but the evaluation of training inputs and learning outputs.

Alan Chambers is often asked by the organizational sponsors of his North Pole trips where he takes executive leaders to the Pole as part of their own development 'Can you give me evidence Alan of what they will learn from this, before we commit to the time and cost of such an approach?' His response is significant: 'I can't tell them what they are going to learn. They need to know before they sign up what their personal reasons are for joining. It will be different for each person.' This tells you something about Alan's views on personal responsibility. The point is the North Pole trip provides the environment where some very powerful learning will take place, but we cannot take a centralist approach expecting to be able to define 'learning outcomes' which will apply to all members equally, ahead of time.

Yet in the corporate world, amongst those charged with the sponsorship or the administration of such events, there is a strong desire to know ahead of time, what the outcomes will be. And because corporates see their human members as a 'resource', it would help if there could be some standardization when dealing with the learning of groups of people. Alan Chambers' point is learning at the level experienced on the North Pole is very personal. Many of the executives who go, have already built massively successful business empires. They have all the recognition, status and money anyone could dream of. They may not even know what it is they are looking to learn ahead of time. It may be that the learning which is achieved emerges through the period of intense action and reflection and through working with other team members from different backgrounds in the radically different environment of the Arctic. Sure there may be technical learning, such as learning how to navigate or how to walk on ice, but to reduce the evaluation of learning to this is missing the point. This point is also often missed in executive development programmes, where more focus is placed on the easier to measure technical or knowledge based learning than personal learning. Often I suspect this need to know what someone else has learnt is about control; yet the most powerful types of learning are deeply personal. Furthermore some people prefer to keep their personal reflections of their learning to themselves. Because they are not disclosing their learning in detail does not mean it is not happening. Indeed it may be that the most powerful learning is that which is not shared. This creates a problem for the learning and development specialist who feels a need to expose the learning in order to be able to measure it so that they can prove their own value, as Kirkpatrick suggests they should.

Myth No. 2 - Courses Prove Learning

Kirkpatrick's statement above implies that scientific and statistical measurement is the best way of proving effectiveness of training. Well, maybe if measuring in an environment where variables can be controlled and where it is possible to isolate cause and effect. He suggests we should use control groups where possible to be able to prove the value of training. Control groups are fine in laboratory conditions but less practicable in most organizational training and particularly leadership development, which aims to have an impact on job performance. If you try to set up a control group there are just too many real life variables to control in order to achieve a valid measure. In the real world of the organization, real life gets in the way of such assessment.

Individuals might be encouraged to present the evidence of their learning. If they can identify realistic before and after measures and if a financial case can be made that there has been a return on investment, then that is important.

However, in the quest for presenting a financial case, all too often qualitative issues are subjected to fabricated and meaningless quantitative formulae.

The centralist quest for standardization and statistical measurement usually ends up as a measurement of inputs rather than outputs. Reports are prepared which show, for example the number of training days delivered, the number of hours spent in the classroom, or the number of courses running. These measures are more defensive and retrospective than strategic; they are designed to show the training department has been doing its job and that it knows how the budget has been spent. They bear no relationship to the measurement of learning or business outcomes.

Alan Chambers in many ways is an action learner. He practises what Reg Revans, doyen of action learning preached. He recognizes that real life on the ice is not a controllable experiment and survival cannot be taught in the classroom. Sure, training events held in the outdoor environment over several weeks, in the run up to the TP2K expedition were vital, in order to instill the basic skills, to develop a mutual understanding and to prepare for every eventuality that could be reasonably anticipated. This in fact saved lives; when Charlie Paton fell through the ice, twice, and the fact that the team had practised the procedure for dealing with this eventuality, clearly was critical. Alan realized, though, that he had to get beyond the classroom; the real learning was to be gained through practice or by getting as close to others who had relevant experience as he could. So he went, on his own, to live with the Inuits in the northern territories of Canada. When asked what he learned from this experience he says:

'I learnt confidence, personal confidence such as what ice was thin enough to walk on. As I was inching gingerly out onto the ice with all my cold weather clothing on, hoping I wouldn't get a cold weather injury and the ice would hold my 12 stone, an Inuit would drive past at 20 miles an hour on a skidoo with no face mask or gloves. Learning how to read the thickness of the ice was my first lesson. There were many lessons, most of them learned with my visual interpretation and learning through watching them work, live and go about their business. In my mind these were priceless lessons that couldn't be taught - just respected and copied. Ignorance out on the ice can be fatal. The Inuit people really respect nature and how powerful the Arctic weather and conditions can be. To disregard their culture would be foolhardy. If I could study new skills with self-assurance and competence then it would help me manage the team members' apprehension and nervousness. Patience was probably the second most important thing to be learned. I learnt this through the way they hunt... standing all day by the side of a ringed seal's air hole in freezing temperatures.

Not losing sight of the bigger picture…whether waiting for an hour or five, the end result had to be achieved.'

Myth No. 3 - Good Course Evaluations Mean Learning

The reactions level (Kirkpatrick level 1) is usually tackled through end of course evaluation questionnaires, and because it is easy to do 78 percent of organizations are evaluating in this way. However this is usually little more than a litmus test for happiness at the time of answering the questions. Happiness does not necessarily mean learning. Often the most powerful learning experiences that people report, come from difficult and painful experiences, such as being thrown in at the deep end with a new job or having to adapt to a new industry.

Post-course evaluation questionnaires may assess the level of happiness of a participant but this must not be confused with evidence of learning. If trainers are aware that they may be judged on the post-course evaluation scores, they soon learn to use applied psychology in ensuring that participants are in a state of pleasure before completing their evaluation forms!

Myth No. 4 – Real Learning Takes Place in the Classroom

Evaluation at the level of learning (Kirkpatrick level 2) concerns the extent to which the learner is able to recall learning after the event. If this concerns knowledge recall this may be easy to assess. However, in organizations the focus of learning is increasingly on skills development and behavioural change. For these aspects of learning the old model does not hold. Such learning is most personal and difficult even for individuals to judge for themselves. I have often been fascinated that when organizations have run follow-up days, say three months after a course, how people will recount learning that was never even covered on the original course. What is happening here is a misattribution of the learning to a particular event.

In terms of behavioural skills and management training it is possible to see short-term changes in capability over a period of classroom based training. This is only part of the learning process though; tackling knowledge and skills over a short period of time. The true test is whether such learning leads to sustained changes in behaviour and leads to action. Many studies have shown the significant attrition rate in learning over an extended period of time.

Over the past few years we have asked over 3,000 leaders about the most significant learning experiences in their lives. None have quoted training courses, business school or classroom based training. The overwhelming majority quote job based experiences, periods of rapid change and specific individuals who have helped accelerate the learning process through effective, and often informal, coaching or mentoring.

This supports the views of Wenger, who suggests that learning is a social process often emergent in communities of practice and through the conveyance of tacit learning. He shows the difficulties in prescribing what will be learnt. Revans, founding father of action learning, has also stressed the significance of managers learning from each other in learning sets. He suggests that real learning comes from insightful questioning about work issues rather than 'programmed knowledge' alone. He says 'there is no learning without action and no action without leaning'.

Myth No. 5 - There is a Direct Correlation Between Management Education and Business Improvement

Many organizations have continued to invest in management education without even attempting to measure the impact on the business. In some cases individuals are allowed to apply for company sponsorship for external education, but there is precious little attempt to engage in discussion about what is being taught and how it can be applied back in the organization. A review of research by Hirsh and Carter into the value of management education and management development reveals some interesting challenges for the future:

- The motivation for management education usually comes from the individual in order to meet personal career needs through achievement of qualifications (for example the business school MBA)

- The management education agenda is driven by a normative model with a predetermined syllabus without input from the business

- There is no evidence of a correlation between attendance on external business education programmes and improved business performance.

How Do We Move Beyond the Myths – Start with Action and Performance

If these are some of the myths that have developed concerning organizational training, then what should we do about it? Maybe to perpetuate the myth is less controversial and problematic than to challenge it. We have spoken to many Training and HR Managers who have shown with pride the suite of training courses that they manage. Yet they often will agree that there is no evidence of a return on investment and that because the courses are isolated off-job events, there is little likelihood of the training having a sustained impact when the participants return to their jobs. They recognize the paradox, but do nothing about it. Furthermore, the same Training managers will bemoan the fact that the business leaders do not value training and development and the same HR Managers will complain that they are not taken seriously at board level.

So here are some suggestions for a new *modus operandi* and a reformulation of the way we should look at evaluation of learning and ensure that leaders are provided with the best opportunities to develop.

Learning is the Responsibility of the Participant

Many HR and Training staff talk about the need to encourage members of their organization to take responsibility for their learning, and there are an increasing number of systems to support this, often linked in with performance management and personal development plans. Introducing documentation and a centrally driven system, however, does not change behaviour and attitudes.

The motivation to take responsibility for your own learning will come from experience, encouragement and most of all from within.

Rather than focus on the roll out of Personal Development Plans we should start with real business issues, and establish work groups which are also learning groups. Participants should be asked to define their personal learning objectives from the start, to review learning at regular intervals and at the end of work based projects. Learning comes from action and learning is a social process. I have been involved with supporting such projects in commercial organizations and in public services. The responsibility for learning can shift psychologically and literally from the training or HR professional to the participant. In order to achieve this you need to establish expectations and ground-rules from the start and then provide supportive and assertive facilitation throughout a defined project and period of action and learning. Strong facilitation and work groups can create a constructive form of peer pressure and a learning culture.

One leader from a major drinks business where we set up such projects described it like this: 'I have been through a taught MBA programme and a number of company courses, but this process has provided the most powerful learning experience so far.' This person had been through a leadership development programme that combined taught inputs and skills development with learning set 'trios' where members supported each other in exploring action plans and learning. One year after the formal programme had finished I met this person who was delighted to report that the 'trio' was still meeting and had moved to another level of understanding and learning insight. In fact he was worried that there were moves from the training department to change the membership of the trio and felt this would be destructive.

When working with extended periods of action and learning in this way, at the end of a defined period, say 100 days, participants can present the value added case to key stakeholders. Colleagues and the organization's leaders should hear about both the actions they have taken and the learning that has occurred. The emphasis should be on what has been done rather than making recommendations for approval.

Proving Learning is Integral to the Process of Learning

Opportunities should be provided for participants on development programmes to write up a summary of their learning and for this to be held as a record of and in recognition of their added value contribution to the business. The sum of all such records will outweigh any attempt centrally to evaluate a training programme with phoney post-course evaluation formulae. The training and development team members will establish higher credibility as the facilitators of business related learning rather than being seen as administrators and systems police.

Learning takes place at various levels as shown in the Model of Learning. In working with real work projects as a basis for learning, this model can be used to emphasise the importance of moving beyond the levels of knowledge acquisition, skills development, and even beyond motivation where you say you are going to implement your learning. It is easy to debate theory or case studies in the classroom or even to play act in role-plays, but it is what people do that counts.

Facilitators of leadership development should keep asking learners questions such as:

- 'What are you going to do about it?'

- 'What have you done?'

- 'What have you learned from your actions?'

These are simple questions but eventually they become stock questions which people ask of each other. There are no hiding places; either you have taken action or you haven't. Individuals should start by reviewing their own actions and learning. They are in the best place to judge their own unique learning experiences.

Learning can be described in quantitative ('I have reduced costs by per fifteen per cent') or qualitative terms ('I have learnt how to adapt my influencing style when dealing with the Chief Executive'). The role of the facilitator is to help individuals and teams define the measures and articulate and share their learning.

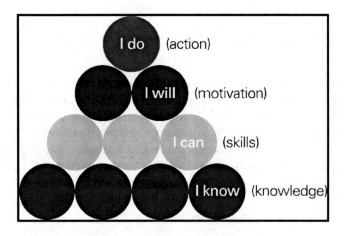

Hale Model of Levels of Learning

The Importance of Reflection

Donald Schön has contributed to the theory of learning and education of relevance to executive development. He has stressed the importance of reflection in the process of learning. He refers to 'reflection-in-action' or 'reflection-on-action.' We can see how this works in Alan Chambers' expeditions. For instance, Alan stops his expedition party at very regular periods, in some cases hourly, when walking on the ice and asks them to review what they are learning; this might be considered to be a form of reflection-in-action. Although he has walked on the ice hundreds of times before, he realizes on every occasion there is something different, he can take nothing for granted and he needs to ensure the party are constantly internalizing learning as the opportunity arises, rather than letting the learning slip away.

Alan also institutes what he calls 'tent time'; this is where at the end of each day the team are asked to reflect on the action from the day, to share their learning and to deal with any niggles, grievances or to raise ideas as to how things could be improved. This is a form of reflection-on-action.

Additionally, Alan sees real value in the maintenance of personal diaries. These are updated at the end of each day. This is a powerful form of personal reflection. He sees the diary serving two purposes. Firstly, it is providing a record for future explorers and adventurers, so is a source of technical data. Secondly, it provides an outlet for personal feelings to be expressed. Often where there are strong emotions being experienced during the day then there needs to be an outlet and there are things which need to be recorded privately in the diary. Interestingly the great modern day explorer and adventurer Sir Ranulph Fiennes in his book Captain Scott, has quite a lot to say about the importance of the diary. He notes how the diaries maintained on the Terra Nova expedition provided valuable meteorological records for the future, but also how they provided an outlet for emotions. He counsels against putting too much emphasis on the negative emotions which are expressed in diaries, particularly towards fellow team members, because he says the extremes which people experience often bring out extreme emotional reactions, which are suppressed in the periods of action but given an outlet through the diary entries. Indeed Fiennes' view is backed up by some of the explorers with, for instance, Titus Oates whose early diary entries and letters to his mother are most critical of their leader Captain Scott. Later in the expedition he advises his readers not to put too much weight on his earlier criticisms; they were simply an outlet at a time of great pressure.

Some of the corporate organizations that Alan Chambers has presented to and most of those that I have worked with, recognize that they do not create an environment where the power of reflection is respected. More often a culture is created of action, where being seen to be active and achieving tasks is respected and rewarded most highly, but reflection, because it is often associated with passive internal processes, is seen as non-productive. In my experience asking executives to keep a reflective diary or log of their learning can be very powerful, and is simple for them to do. However, reflection need not always be an individual process, it can be done collaboratively. Indeed, some organizations who have heard Alan Chambers speak, have instituted organizational or departmental 'tent time' when they reflect on learning from the day or week, and they incorporate their learning into future plans and actions.

A Coach or Mentor Connects Learning with Action

If we accept the limitations of off-job courses in leading to sustained behaviour changes, what else should be done to support learning at a level deeper than knowledge and skills acquisition? There has been a growth in coaching and mentoring over recent years and I researched the impact of mentoring upon learning as a focus for my doctoral research. Effective mentoring can be seen as the missing link between off job training and action in the workplace.

Here are some quotations from people who have described how mentoring helped them achieve insights:

'I came to understand why my approach sometimes does not have the desired effect. These insights came from my mentor challenging me to question my style and way of working.'

'I got an opportunity to discuss how she (mentor) handles people management issues such as discipline and personal issues - we would go through what if scenarios.'

'I have completed a College Diploma but it is good to be working with someone who is very influential in affecting the direction of the business and seeing how they think and operate.'

It was clear from the research I have conducted into mentoring that it is able to help in the development of self-confidence, where the mentor would push the person they were mentoring into action where they may have otherwise been reticent. Such confidence would build through effective preparation and debriefing. Additionally a good mentor was able to help the individual make connections between skills developed through off-job courses and application in the real job situation.

It was clear that mentoring could help the development of insights. Insights begin more with the individual, emerge for the individual, assisted by the effective mentor, and are personal. The development of insights is less plannable than course-based skills development. Whether or not they emerge will depend on real-life circumstances and experiences.

Views and Experiences of the Mentor Current Past	**Workings of the Organisation**
Self-Insight Through Self-questioning	**Workings of Senior Managers**

How Mentors Support Learning Insights
Hale Doctoral Research, 2000

The role of HR and Training departments should be to facilitate rather than control mentoring relationships. Organizations, often with the best intentions, try to engineer such relationships by forcing people into a mentoring 'system', rather than facilitating and supporting good mentoring. Similarly with the growth of centrally driven coaching 'systems', there are often attempts to systematize relationships rather than create a culture where they can flourish. Ironically, in attempts to set up formal coaching and mentoring, it is easy to ignore or fail to see some of the best coaching and mentoring relationships that have already developed informally within the business.

Align Education and Accreditation with Real Leadership Challenges

Henry Mintzberg in his book *Managers Not MBAs*, provides a powerful critique of the case method which has become the most used method for executive development. I have over the past five years been working with major corporations that are using a different method as the basis for leadership development and education called Leadership Questions (LQ). This approach builds an accredited Masters degree around LQs which are focused around specific business problems or issues. There is no syllabus in a traditional sense; participants define the syllabus by scoping the terms of reference for LQs which are then researched and addressed through action in the business.

For instance LQs have addressed such issues as:

- Reducing costs
- Achieving increased employee engagement
- Managing the integration of two business departments
- Increasing sales performance in a specific product line and region
- Improving customer satisfaction.

Participants are grouped into learning sets and meet together regularly to support each other, using insightful questioning and action learning processes. The aim is that participants as real leaders are able to take better informed actions and reflect on their learning. This approach has been received with tremendous enthusiasm by organizations interested in leadership development due to the fact it hits strategy relevant business objectives, whilst motivating participants to learn from their action. This may sound simple, but sadly the business education system on both sides of the Atlantic has until recently ingrained a different approach. Mintzberg says,

'Management is not a science or profession but a practice which calls for a blend of science, art and craft.'

I would agree. We encourage participants to address the messiness of managerial and leadership problems. This means sometimes using scientific methods and approaches but also managing politics on the ground. They legitimately discuss how they have managed the 'politics'; it is not a dirty word.

Mintzberg notes that the traditional approach to management education takes the wrong people who are not managing real situations. Harvard's approach was to develop the case method starting in 1912. The focus is, and remains, on faculty writing cases up according to a set format. Then there is a fixed method for students reading them, analyzing, then debating with the professor who chairs the discussion, with students competing for his or her attention, and being assessed for their contribution. There is a known 'correct' range of issues to be debated and identified by the analysis of the students. There is with the case method an incorrect assumption that it is developing the capability of managers to manage in real business situations. Given many of the graduates of these programmes have gone into business it has led to a domination of an analytical approach to strategy in organizations. This has been at the expense of spontaneity and creativity in strategy formulation.

A requirement for anyone working on one of our programmes is they have to be working as managers and leaders in real jobs in real organizations. I would agree with Mintzberg that to really learn about leadership, you have to do it. It is not an academic subject for objective study, it involves doing. I recently visited a business school where hundreds of students were pouring out of the exam halls comparing notes on how they had tackled their exam questions on business issues. The discussions centred around whether the correct theories had been referred to. None were working in business as they were all full time students, and the professor I was meeting was unaware of how many students were going into business.

This reminded me of the comment from a colleague who supervises full-time Masters students. Once of his best academic students, who had achieved a distinction in her Masters had recently started work in a consultancy organization. Excited and wide-eyed as she entered the world of work her first week in business came as something of a shock. She called my colleague and said she was finding it difficult to know how to tackle her first project because she did not know which theory to apply.

The Business School academics going right back to Wharton in the 1880s with roots based on a Prussian influence, were critical of 'learning by doing' and based everything around an academic curriculum (accounting, law, economics, finance, and statistics). The impetus for business school programmes in the early 20th Century was coming from academics without first hand experience of business.

I believe the academic disciplines are important, but only in as much as they help inform thinking and action on the ground. We encourage participants on our leadership education programmes to define practical business or leadership questions and then search the literature or other organizations for ideas, principles and sources of comparison. Most leadership problems are multi-faceted in terms of academic disciplines. Take, for instance, the challenge of motivating team members in a newly formed merger of departments. This challenge has a finance dimension, as there will be costs and savings associated with such a merger. There will be a psychological dimension as participants will have different personal feelings and there will be a sociological dimension as people are tribal and need to adapt to working on new groups and teams. However, to study these subjects in isolation and say: 'I am now going to do the finance and then I am going to do the psychology' would not work. Leaders need to be adept at working with multi-disciplinary problems.

Harvard have never been able to address the issue of what Mintzberg calls 'soft skills' such as leadership and ethics, with these being added in as classes. I believe leadership is not just another topic to be studied in a busines school class. It is a theme which threads its way through all of the LQs tackled by participants on the programmes we run. Leaders should be encouraged to think through what their personal and overarching objective is in terms of leadership development. This will be different for different leaders. For example, one leader may want to develop a breadth of experience so she is more marketable for career advancement in their industry. Another may want to improve his ability to communicate effectively on issues of business strategy. Once these personal objectives have been defined, then LQs can be scoped in order to provide opportunities to develop these capabilities.

Traditionally, Business School programmes may have helped individual employment propositions, but they do not necessarily lead to improved business performance. The time has come to challenge the old thinking that Business Schools are the owners and protectors of business knowledge and content. Given the accelerating rate of change, managers working on real business challenges in their organizations are often facing challenges that have never been faced before. Anywhere. Rather than send managers to the Business School, we need to invite the Business Schools in to look at the real business challenges faced in the business and ensure they work collaboratively on the business agenda. Organizations should not allow Business Schools to hijack the internal management agenda with their own predefined syllabus, faculty and content-led programmes.

A Call to Action for Learning and Development Specialists

1. Make participants responsible for identifying and consulting the stakeholders who stand to benefit from training and development they are taking part in.

2. Encourage them to identify how they are currently adding value for themselves, their job, team and organization before, during and after a training and development process.

3. Help them to capture learning that is taking place in the job situation through effective facilitation, learning logs and peer learning sets.

4. Transform the training department from a team of officers and administrators into a team of consultants and facilitators with the political and business skills to oil the wheels of learning.

5. Ensure trainers practise what they preach by sharing their learning based on their work activities.

6. Support informal learning processes such as coaching and mentoring without introducing rules, forced relationships and bureaucracy.

7. Interchange people between staff HR and Training functions and business functions.

8. Establish a system of evaluation through accreditation that assesses outputs from learning, not just inputs.

9. Identify the vital business questions that should be tackled, and support individuals and teams in tacking these questions.

10. Keep asking others and yourself how they/you are adding value at a personal, team and organizational level.

7 - Leadership Perspectives

This chapter is based on a number of interviews Richard Hale held with Alan Chambers in order to develop an understanding of Alan's approach to leadership and his views on different dimensions of leadership. Richard also contributes his views on certain aspects of leadership and learning based on his interest in the development of corporate leaders.

- On Management and Leadership -

RIH: I have found it interesting to ask corporate leaders on leadership programmes what their approach to leadership is and what are their beliefs about leadership. Usually the respondents stumble over their words and play for time. Yet they carry the title leader and they are on a programme to develop as leaders. It is as though they are comfortable studying leadership as a subject - something to be looked at objectively - but they do not actually see themselves as leaders. Leadership is not part of their self-concept. It is fine to study great leaders and decide which ones you admire, but these are iconic leaders, distant and remote from the reality of the problems of leading in the everyday hubbub of the corporation. In truth many of these organizational leaders still see themselves as and are still working primarily as managers. Kotter has made a useful distinction between leadership and management, saying that leadership is primarily about planning, budgeting, organizing, staffing, controlling and problem solving. This he says produces predictability, and short term results. Leadership, he says, is about establishing direction, developing a vision and aligning people, motivating and inspiring them. This can produce dramatic change. Of course it is not about either/or; you can be a leader and at times have to manage as well. Culturally, business schools have reinforced this emphasis on management over and above leadership. The MBA focuses on business 'administration' not leadership, and there are even some programmes where leadership does not even feature on the syllabus.

Perhaps it is because management is easier to teach, less nebulous and ill-defined. I would agree that you cannot really 'teach' leadership as such. It is not a topic that can be reduced to tools and techniques. It is more than that. Whilst we search for the one model of leadership or the iconic leader to emulate, in reality leadership is a messy and unpredictable business. It involves both taking the high ground and being able to look to the future, being able to visualize it and to inspire people to buy into this vision. Yet at the same time, it involves working on the ground with the challenges of dealing with different personalities, coping with and becoming part of the organizational politics. There are no hard and fast rules; there is no formula that will guarantee success. There is not even one right answer as to what constitutes great leadership. He or she who is a great leader to one person may be a quite the opposite to another person. Arguably leadership is a 'social construct'. It is a concept we have created, rather than an entity.

We have seen a number of trends in the study of leadership and the literature on the subject. The 'great man' theories looked at those considered to be great leaders, in the hope that we would be able to identify common traits, which we could then emulate. This was inconclusive. Then we moved to the idea of situational leadership, accepting that 'different strokes were appropriate for different folks.' This approach makes sense by advising that we should consider the maturity of the 'follower' and adapt our style of leadership accordingly, taking more of a directive approach when appropriate but empowering when the follower is more mature.

However, what do you do when the enormity of the challenge is just too much for the leader to take on alone? Alan Chambers made every member of the team he led to the North Pole in 2000, a leader. They all would take a leg of the journey or a section of the day in the leadership role. Different people demonstrate different strengths as leaders. There is not one formula.

In his book *Captain Scott*, Ranulph Fiennes describes how he has led teams on polar expeditions where the team members are accomplished leaders in their own right. They would often have open debates expressing different views on how things should be done and arguing for a different position than that presented by Fiennes. Fiennes felt this was vital rather than having behind-the-back murmurings. One also can see in his book how Scott would take a situational approach in his own leadership. Scott would at times encourage open debate, but would then as the overall leader make a decision which he expected the group to comply with. There are many references to behind-the-back discussions between those team members who were critical of their leader in particular involving Titus Oates, who was in charge of the ponies on the *Terra Nova* expedition. However, Fiennes is quite clear in his view that one should not place too much emphasis on the negative comments from Oates about Scott in his diary and letters home. He recognizes that under extreme pressure team members need an outlet to express their emotions and often these are exaggerated or exacerbated by the immediate circumstances. Fiennes also refers to the views of Dr Phillip Law, Director of Australia's DEA Antarctic Division who wrote in the 1980s on the qualities of leadership and effective teams:

'One quality is fundamentally essential to any team. It is loyalty. A man must be loyal to the expedition, loyal to his leader and loyal to himself. Some men are naturally loyal; some are fundamentally antagonistic, critically outspoken and disloyal.'

In the leadership programmes we run with corporate organizations we focus on Leadership Questions. The issues that leaders in the business see as important for the future are defined in consultation with stakeholders. These are other people who are interested in the leader succeeding. This may be their own boss, peers or customers or clients. It is the real thorny leadership problem defined as a question which provides the basis for investigation and action. It is the research and action which provides the basis for the demonstration of leadership capabilities.

Many organizations have taken a centralist approach to defining the capabilities or competencies of a successful leader. Organizational systems of assessment and measurement of leaders are structured around these normative models and HR professionals wrestle with the dentitions and language, trying to work out what leadership looks like at different levels. Our approach is to start at the other end, with the problems and opportunities on the ground. Leaders tackle these, and in the process have an opportunity to demonstrate effective leadership as assessed by the people who really count, the followers or team members who they are leading. They are then able to bring the leadership capability framework alive by demonstrating in a very real way how they have shown effective leadership, and how others have evaluated their contribution. In this way I believe organizations are better able to define leadership, based on reality, on actual activity, rather than by trying to define a central model and then force it down through the organization.

RIH: *Can you define, measure and assess leadership?*

AWC: Leadership is different for everyone – there is definitely not one model. I have to manage individuals differently to get 100 percent from the team. I still want an end result of 100 percent. I home in on the inner qualities of people; their passion rather than their CV, or what courses they have been on.

RIH: *On the 2000 expedition it was Charlie who finished the actual walk with you. He had never put on a pair of skis before the trip. What were the qualities you saw in him?*

AWC: I think it was commitment. He must have thought long and hard about this trip before committing to it. It wasn't just physical, there was a big commitment in terms of preparation organizationally, academically, and logistically. Charlie is very physically minded, there would have been an appeal for him in testing himself physically and skiing was just a skill he needed to learn. Also, he had a huge desire to learn. He wanted to be able to lead trips after he came back and he is now leading his own trips. He had a massive hunger for learning. He had that willingness to constantly improve and become a bigger player. My role was to change the way he thought – he was a weakness at the start as he was too fit; he had no body fat. I had to change the way he was operating. Trying to tell a guy who had spent four hours a day for the last 10 years in the gym to stop doing this was hard.

He had a very practical approach to problem solving whereas my approach would be to contingency plan. It would have been easy for me to say I know what to do, but I gave him the opportunity to present ideas and to go live with them. It didn't feel risky to do this because I believe that not one person can lead the team. On the ice I needed people from the team to lead; one to save my energy, but also to keep them engaged. All members would lead legs of the trip, deciding from the front on what we should do, picking and selecting a route, deciding when to stop and go and keeping an eye on the group. This was about keeping the project alive, it was our project, not just Alan's project. Some people did emerge as strong leaders on the ice – Charlie was one, as he would do more than the minimum that was required. There are some people who work out what the minimum is and do that. They get by, but they are not exceptional leaders.

RIH: *How do you think you operate as a leader?*

AWC: I think I am confident in the way I try to get the best out of people. I don't like wasting time. Sometimes this is a downside. I confront straight away. I created the overall vision for the 2000 Expedition. Having committed to it personally I had to get other people to buy into it.

There had to be a leader for administrative reasons and to play the system however I wasn't the highest rank. Just because of rank you shouldn't assume a greater level of knowledge and specific experience. I believe the right way to operate and manage the team was to utilize everyone's different level of experience knowledge, thinking and ideas. Not one person held all the answers and could make all the decisions that would get us to the North Pole. However, one person could organize the process, so that's where the leadership element came in. So I suppose the strategy was to draw on everyone's experience and knowledge but direct it in the most positive and useful way through a decision-maker/spokesperson which was ultimately me.

RIH: Scott talks of the 'extreme togetherness' - how this bonded the team - also of his black dog moods and depressions - what was your experience of how relationships developed on your 2000 expedition and how close you got to understanding others and their personalities?

AWC: I didn't really know the true people until we were at our most extreme temperatures. The penetrating deathly cold brought out traits and characteristics that I had never seen before in the team. Also the cold suppressed some of the great qualities that were present in everyone when we were in training in a controlled environment. I forged a close relationship with Charlie very early on the ice. Because of his fitness supremacy over the team I knew he would struggle with the cold so I was very aware that he would need me to support him without singling him out. It may be just an extra piece of chocolate at the end of the day from my rations. Or thinking that he is feeling more tired than the rest of us; then I'd give him a task in the tent straight away in the warmth where he would be out of the elements which would help him personally and emotionally while the rest of us worked on securing the tent and doing the night time outside jobs. The longer the trip went on the more the purgatory set in, the mental attitudes of people developed and changed and at one point I became quite a lonely leader.

RIH: What is your view on the idea of heroic leaders?

AWC: I don't like the word hero associated with me. It implies there is more risk than there was for those people I see as heroic leaders. I think our bravery came from making the personal choice to do the trip in the first place. Some people love the word and like to be seen as heroes. I look up to Sir Ernest Shackleton and Captain Scott as heroes. Look at Sir Ranulph Fiennes, it is incredible what he has attempted, I don't think anyone will come close to achieving a fraction of what he has achieved with complete commitment. But it is the old explorers in history I also admire, as true heroes. They would wave goodbye to their wives and loved ones saying 'I'll see you in a couple of years' and they did not know what was out there then. We now know what is out there.

RIH: Many of the leadership development programmes I have been involved in are linked to qualifications, some up to Masters degree level. However they are different to the traditional MBA type programme where you study specific subjects at particular times during the academic year. I am very interested in the ideas of Henry Mintzberg who in his book *Managers Not MBAs* gives an excellent account of the development of the business education system. He notes the powerful influence of the case method in determining how leaders in organizations think and tackle problems. He argues that case studies are an intellectual game, where the professor knows the answer, what actually happened in an historic case, and the challenge is for students to outwit each other and work out what the answer is. He is also very critical of the 'factory' approach to the production of case studies, with professors competing to see who can write the most or the best cases each academic year. Mintzberg extrapolates from this that as many of the graduates of the traditional Business School MBA programmes, who have been schooled in the case method, then go onto senior roles determining the strategy of major organizations, they take this case study mentality with them. This he believes has led to an over-emphasis on analysis in the formation of strategy.

This is significant given Mintzberg is talking from a base of considerable experience working within the North American business school tradition. He has clearly become frustrated with the emphasis on intellectual problem solving through the case method over and above action. There are parallels here with the views of Reg Revans on action learning; he promoted the idea that action should lead to learning, and was critical of the idea of starting in the classroom. Often I hear managers and leaders comparing notes with one another on their management education. 'Where did you take your MBA?' they ask, whereas I think this is the wrong question. More appropriate would be 'What did you learn as a result of your MBA and what have you done as a result?'

With the Leadership Questions method, we start by asking the organization and the leaders within it to define the key questions which are critical for future success. Indeed we encourage them to go and ask other stakeholders in the business how they see the problem or question. So the question emerges from the business, not from the business school. This may sound simple but it represents a critical difference, educationally and philosophically, from the way business education has traditionally been conducted. The business and the leaders actually define the syllabus and the cases are real live cases from within the organization, which need to be tackled or which have been quietly ignored because they are seen as too tough to tackle. Having defined the critical questions, then workshops and learning set group discussions can focus on what is critical for the business. If organizational change is the crunch issue currently because of a recent or imminent takeover, then the workshop focuses on that. Theoretical models and concepts can be brought in to support the workshop, but an absolute requirement is to move beyond a talking shop. Leaders on such programmes have to do what leaders are supposed to do, take action and learn from it. Furthermore, assessment and ultimate success academically is based on a requirement to demonstrate how the question was formulated, what the learning set contributed, what action has been taken and what has been learnt.

For many leaders in organizations they find this process at first uncomfortable. I believe this is often because they have become conditioned to viewing education as a passive process where you are taught by a teacher who has knowledge to impart. There is a need to redefine what constitutes learning; to unlearn about learning, before learning about learning. Initially on such programmes they may become frustrated, expecting that there should be more academic input, but in most cases they come to realize through experience that the action learning based approach is in fact more empowering.

Such an approach challenges the facilitators of action learning based education programmes too. With the traditional model of business education, the faculty holds the trump cards. They have the knowledge, know the answers to the case studies, and control the assessment. There is a dependency relationship between 'student' and faculty; albeit the student may be controlling millions of spend and leading thousands of people. With the action learning model, the challenge for the facilitator is specifically not to create a dependency relationship, but to help the learner to take responsibility for their own learning. I have seen many faculty members struggle with this, often feeling they are not adding value unless they bring along to a workshop session or a set meeting a few 'tricks of the trade' in terms of process techniques or some special knowledge that only they knew up until the point they reveal it to the group. I would rather they bring along their ability to ask insightful questions and to stimulate a spirit of inquiry and to model the behaviours of action learning.

So, I do believe formal education can add real value to the development of leaders, but when it is delivered or facilitated in an action learning way. I recall the MD of a bank saying that as a boy he saw little in school education for him, because he did not know how to apply it. After he joined a bank as a school leaver, he could see a potential future and therefore had a reason to study, which he did successfully by applying his learning to real life and work and so he was able to climb to the top of the organization.

In a similar way the famous explorer Sir Ernest Shackleton was by his own admission no star at school, but he was a star scholar once he had a purpose and goal, that was once he had decided he would become an expert seaman. Education makes sense for people when they know the purpose.

RIH: *What has been your own experience of education?*

AWC: I went to a traditional comprehensive school in the North East of England. I found it difficult that I had to choose subjects at a young age. I liked geography and history – but there was a clash on the timetable so I couldn't follow my interest. I enjoyed the sport side. I did well in my subjects at school but I did not turn up to the exams and sit them. By the time it came to the exams I knew I wanted to join the Royal Marines. Once I had found out I had got in I felt I didn't need the exams. I had a purpose and knew what I wanted to do. I left school at 16 and three weeks later joined the Royal Marines. 54 of us started and six of us finished – I had to have a deep purpose to put myself through that. But then I constantly challenged myself through my time in the Marines. Even though it was extremely strenuous, I started to look to that extra challenge away from the Marines – and I got the feel for working in the cold.

- On Innovation -

RIH: Many of the organizations I work with talk about the need to be innovative. One company I worked with on a consultancy basis asked if I would join a group which had been set up as a think tank in order to make recommendations on how the business should become more innovative. It was an organization with many time served employees and was certainly a conservative culture. Maybe the senior director who sponsored this project realized that without innovation there was a real risk that more agile competitors would come in and steal market share and undermine the business. The group undertook some 'industrial tourism' where they went out and studied how other organizations encourage innovation and then were thinking about how they could present their findings back to their sponsors. The chair of the group was most worried that he could not think of an innovative way of presenting, other than providing multi-coloured binders in which to present the written report to their audience. Frustrated with the challenge he said to me with resignation 'Well I guess it was not part of the brief that we had to be innovative in how we went about our research.' Really he was saying it was ok to study innovation and make recommendations; if his group just did this, he will have fulfilled the brief. In terms of leadership he was not ever going to go the extra mile, to do more than was required in the brief. It is this quality of doing more than is required which Alan Chambers associates with the outstanding leaders he has worked and walked with.

In the same organization I was a member of a group with a number of the internal directors, responsible for governing the education programmes for managers and leaders within the business. I was presenting the benefits of the Leadership Question approach and explaining how the middle managers were gaining a great deal from using this approach to research and their own personal development. I suggested they might like to consider introducing such an approach for the senior directors of the organization. The room fell silent. Then one of the directors turned to me and asked, 'Which other organizations have their directors doing Leadership Questions?' 'None… yet.' I replied. The director looked at me with a slightly embarrassed smile and then said wryly, 'Ah ha so we would be the first… innovation eh!' The decision was then swiftly made that it perhaps would not be appropriate to introduce such an innovative approach for the senior directors as they would be far too busy, but it was fine to encourage it amongst the middle managers.

I see innovation as a relative concept rather than an absolute. For a very conservative organization with an entrenched conservative culture, simply to move managers out of their offices may be considered to be a considerable innovation. For an external observer from an organization that thrives on innovation this may be seen as a fairly conservative act.

Alan Chambers looks to the early polar explorers as great innovators and seeks to innovate himself as can seen below. One does sense a period of innovation as the new polar routes were being discovered. For instance Scott in his *Endurance* and *Terra Nova* expeditions was constantly learning from experience and testing new theories and approaches. Certainly he sought to learn from the innovations of others, for instance the use of dogs and skis by the Norwegians, but he was willing to take unproven approaches and try them out in practice. For instance, there was no certain cure for scurvy but there were unproven preventative ideas such as eating fresh meat; Scott ordered big supplies of mutton for his trips and he sent out hunting groups to search for seals and penguins.

What is now labelled as Seasonal Affective Disorder, a form of depression triggered by periods of physical darkness, was not clearly defined in Scott's time. However, some explorers had started to experiment with lighting systems to alleviate these effects. Scott set up a system of candles and lanterns and a windmill based electric lighting system to keep his ship lit during periods of extended darkness in the Antarctic.

Scott experimented with a hydrogen balloon in which men ascended 600 feet in order to gain a view into uncharted territory; this was in effect the first manned flight in the Antarctic.

Scott also experimented with the first motorized sledges, with continuous tracks, which were the forerunners of the military tank

RIH: *Do you learn from case studies of other explorers or leaders?*

AWC: I do learn from others. I studied meticulously how other explorers and adventurers have approached the North Pole, and I looked at what they did and how they did it, what equipment they took, what diet they used and suchlike. However, I always questioned what they did, and because no-one had done specifically what we were aiming to do, I could only use this previous experience of others to a limited extent. I had to challenge what they did and look for the weaknesses in their approach, and to innovate, to think of a different way of doing it. I also could not just rely on studying what others had done academically. I used the study of what they did to help formulate a theory of how we should do it. I tested this out in various ways, such as by going to the North Pole on my own and testing out different types of clothing. I also realized that there was a lot to be gained by talking to other people, both other explorers and those who were used to living on the ice, such as the Inuits. So I went and lived with them. I conducted my research by becoming part of their group on a regular trip each year in preparation for the Team Polar 2000 expedition.

- On Learning -

RIH: I find it helpful to describe learning as taking place at different levels. Some time ago training specialists used to focus on providing training at the levels of:

- Knowledge
- Skills
- Attitudes.

In other words they would try to design training in such a way it would provide change at these three levels. Clearly, knowledge and skills are relatively straightforward to develop assuming appropriate ability or aptitude exists within the learner. You can provide books or lectures to develop knowledge. However, possessing the knowledge of something, say how to delegate effectively, does not necessarily give you the skills to do it. You might know that effective delegation is a key competence of effective leaders, and you might be able to describe the steps of delegation, but this does not mean you have the skills to delegate effectively. Skills can be developed in a training course situation or on the job through practice. Attitudes, though, were the stumbling block in this model. Trainers found it very difficult to define, instill and measure attitudes. Indeed some would say that in today's organization the idea of controlling attitudes smacks of *big brother*. I take the view that attitudes are personal, not to be controlled by the trainer. My own supervisor for my doctoral research was Alan Mumford, a specialist and authority in area of learning in the organizational context. He told me not to worry about trying to measure attitudes, he preferred the concept of *insights*. I took this message on board and find it helpful to encourage leaders, when thinking about their own learning or that of others they are helping to develop, to consider what insights, or wisdom they are gaining from their experience or observation of others around them. Sometimes an insight comes from piecing together observations with problems and experience. For instance if you are struggling to understand how best to integrate people into a new team (*the problem*) you might gain insights by observing how this is done by a colleague successfully in another part of your business (*observation*) combined with realizing that the method you recently tried seemed to fail (*experience*).

I advocate the use of Learning Logs where you make a note simply of what happened and what your feelings and reflections are. There are various structures you can use for a learning log, the main advice being to keep it simple. You might list in three columns what you intend to stop, start or continue doing as a result of your reflections. The purpose is to capture learning opportunities shortly after an event and to make notes for future records. If you get into the habit of this then you can often achieve an even higher level of learning when you go back to your notes some time afterwards and reflect on your experience and your observations from the past. Donald Schön has researched the concepts of reflection in action and reflection on action which distinguishes well between the idea of reflecting in the moment as things are happening and reflecting after the event.

Most of the leadership development programmes I am involved with are underpinned by the concept of action learning. This involves leaders learning with and from each other in learning groups of about five to eight people with support from an action learning facilitator. A key influence here has been Dr Reg Revans who coined the phrase action learning, following his work with

Nobel Prize-winning scientists at the Cavendish laboratories, and subsequently with the coal industry and health service on the UK and then with industry and academia in Belgium. Revans believed that real learning meant working on real work based problems. He was dismissive of taught courses in management and critical of the idea of the consultant or teacher as a supposed expert. He proposed leading with the business question or problem, and using this as the basis for action and learning. He stressed the importance of asking insightful questions which led to insights; he distinguished wisdom from 'cleverness' or knowledge in isolation from action. It is the importance of action which I like to promote in my model of levels of learning, which shows that learning involves working at all four levels; acquiring knowledge and skills plus having the motivation to take action, and ultimately taking it. I have met many budding leaders who have good knowledge of the key skills and qualities of an effective leader, they are comfortable talking about the theory of leadership but they don't act upon it.

RIH: *How do you approach your own personal learning?*

AWC: I have learnt from my own mistakes, I have also learnt a lot from testing myself physically, mentally and emotionally, more so than a lot of the leaders I have met. I probably push myself physically and mentally more because I need the skills and confidence needed to put a team together. I learnt a lot from being led and also learnt a lot from bad leaders. A lot is on reflection because I feel I need to have the skills to do something before I actually teach it to other people. I feel I have to be confident that I know that I can put up a tent in -50°C in a blizzard so that I am in a position to be able to teach others to do the same. I test myself often on my own. I actually go out into the theatre and put myself through extreme situations so that I know that I am able to go out into those situations with my team feeling confident as a leader. I have learnt a lot from good leaders who I observe and admire. I ask myself the question do I act like that. I also learn a lot from bad leaders by observing how they behave, how they treat other people, how they fail to engage people. I say to myself I never want to lead people in that sort of way.

A lot of the learning that I do as a leader is on reflection, after the here and now. When I have come back from Canada and I am sitting down thinking about what I did and how I did it, I consider what I have learnt and what could I do differently. I also take time out with the team to rehearse situations that I have experienced on my own when I have been out to Canada, even if this means taking half a day out with the team to mimic situations and discuss how they would handle them.

RIH: *How do you go about reflection?*

AWC: It is mostly in note format. I keep a note pad and a diary. I make notes regularly; typically we would stop on a hike every two hours. I would use this time to take a drink, reflect on what we had just experienced, to take notes of learning and ideas. I feel it is important to capture these thoughts and ideas in real time. If you wait until the end of the day, often you can't recall your experiences so clearly. Also if I have an idea, rather than wait to share it with the team at the end of the day I prefer to share it with the team at the time while it is fresh in my mind. Sharing it with the team means that, say, four people are more likely to remember it rather than just me trying to remember it at the end of the day. Also, at the end of the day when we are in the tent for several hours having to melt ice, this is when we as a team discuss some of the ideas that have occurred earlier in the day. Having some time to reflect like this is very valuable

RIH: *With the amount of experience you have, having been on so many expeditions and trips to the Canadian High Arctic a lot of people would say that you must know what to expect, so what is there really for you to continue to learn. So is this process of reflection still really that important?*

AWC: Well, there are certain things that are definites in terms of technical knowledge that I can use, for instance the reading of the ice, the core navigation that will never change. However, you can make the journey more enjoyable and easier if you are continually improving the way in which you do things, for instance by using the latest technology, or innovating with equipment and clothing. It took me ten years to develop the knowledge of what was required in terms of garments. Ten years of experimenting and going back to manufacturers and testing different variations before I could say I had really cracked it. I have actually influenced the manufacturers to innovate in the design of clothing which is relevant in a very practical sense for explorers rather than urban designer outdoor wear. The innovation comes from my own practical experience and the trials and tests that we do on the ice. As an example we realized that we needed a particular type of outer coat which came down below the knees and protected the upper legs from cold. This was not on the public market and certainly would not have been fashionable or attractive to look at, but it was a design that we knew was needed. I keep going back to manufacturers and seeking improvements to equipment. Take the sledge for instance; they had always been square fronted, and you keep getting fractures on the corners. They kept knocking and getting stuck, so we developed the idea of the round fronted bottlenose sledge, which has now become the norm. This is more accessible going through the ice blocks. Everyone else previously had put up with the problem, so they would be having to stop and start 50 times a day whereas we would stop five times a day – well that's 45 times a day you have stopped that I haven't. If you add that over 60 days it is about four days' walking. So you become more efficient. That is of benefit not just for us but for every sledge user, worldwide.

RIH: *A lot of organizations talk about risk management, what is your own approach to risk?*

AWC: I have always approached the management of risk through preparation and by embracing it. I do the correct level of research and reduce the risk but I realize we have to share the research with the rest of the team and show how we are managing risk. This gives reassurance for the team. I take nothing for granted. I don't take for granted that a top sleeping bag will work at -50°C – I make no assumptions. I take it out and test it. It could be that it is a marketing ploy to say it will work at these temperatures. You have to test it as part of your preparation. If I test everything out it is less for the rest of the team to worry about. I do a lot of risk assessment.

In 2000 the whole expedition was at risk and I radioed back to the UK. We were facing a lot of adversity, we were not hitting our schedule, a lot our research had gone out of the window, and the ice flow had taken us off track. A lot of people at base and in the UK felt we might be at risk and would need pulling out. But one of the things Charlie and I would always ask each other was are we able physically and mentally to carry on. If the answer from both of us was yes then we would continue and plan around the adversity. We would come up with a different or revised plan. We would reduce the weight, increase the pace, and rearrange the stores between the sledges. A lot of people expect you to give up. Also, as you have pushed yourself more than you have ever done before there is a risk you don't think so clearly, with sleep deprivation. The fact we were reviewing so regularly meant that we stayed grounded and realistic. We reviewed what we did that hour, that phase, that stage, this kept us grounded. Back home they were asking if we wanted to continue. I said 'we are focused but not blinkered' and because of two things, trust and honesty, this kept the trip going forward. Our man in the UK, Paddy George, knew I was being absolutely honest and if I felt we couldn't make it we would put our hands up.

RIH: *So where did strategy fit in?*

AWC: The strategy came from just one goal. We worked back from there. It was a simple goal to define but there were lots of things that would alter, twist and reshape the plan in order for us to be able to achieve it. But the strategy and planning meant constantly working back from the day we wanted to be stood on the top of the planet. It was as much a backward as a forward based plan. Everything was done to a timeline. The plan alters, though. We were also conditioned by the weather and the time of year, we knew the parameters we had to work in so we knew we had to work within these. We did micro-plan as a team, taking into account everyone's physical ability, levels of experience, and we set our goals from a team perspective. We set our goals in a realistic way and this eradicated a lot of doubt. This kept our plan real and gave confidence to team members who knew they could achieve what was being asked of them. The positive energy at the point we left for the expedition was immense. We approached the plan from the team's perspective, not the leader's aspirations, and we planned together.

RIH: I find that if we talk about research on leadership development programmes, this conjures up images of academia or the research scientist. Research in relation to leadership and improvement in the organizational or business context need not be academic in the sense of pure scientific research; however, there is something to be learned from the discipline associated with research. I see a key role for leaders in researching business challenges which relates to the future success of the organization. Such business issues should be considered as problems rather than puzzles, in that they do not have an absolutely right or wrong answer, and there may be many pathways towards a solution. These are the questions or problems which the board may be aware of in the back of their mind, but they are often avoided or left on the 'too hard to tackle' list. One of the roles of an effective leader is to tackle such questions. Below are some of the issues that I have seen leaders tackle in organizations using the Leadership Questions approach:

- How can we develop our product and service range in such a way that we manage risks associated with smaller, more agile competitors stealing market share?

- How can we create efficiencies based on the integration of currently dispersed services into a shared service centre facility?

- How do we increase sales of financial service products at the same time as improving our effectiveness in collections?

- How do we improve the perception of our customer service competence?

- How do we improve staff retention and engagement?

- How can we prevent those managers in our organization who are identified as having high potential, from becoming 'derailed'?

Such questions are complex, there are many variables, and you cannot work out an answer through a controlled scientific experiment. A leader who is tackling such questions also needs to recognize the social context and political nature of the questions. There will be many different views on how to tackle the problem, and different stakeholders with varying degrees of political power. It might be possible to work out an elegant proposal, but if you are unable to gain political acceptance in the organizational context then it is worthless.

So leaders as practitioner researchers should involve others who are the real players in the organization as apart of their research. This may sound obvious but often senior leaders will feel vulnerable in consulting those people in their organization who are more junior and asking, 'What do you think the problem is? What do you think we should do?'

It is as though this would be admitting weakness because leaders should know the answers. However, Reg Revans in his early work using action learning in the health service found that often the nurses in the hospitals had insights and understanding beyond that of the doctors and more senior health professionals. The matrons would dismiss the nurses as 'ignorant young sluts', yet Revans realized that by allowing them to work together to tackle the significant problems of clinical care and hospital management, they would often achieve much more than their seniors. Good practical research means asking those who are close to the action what they see and what they think.

One important aspect of research is the use of comparison. One could take any of the problems listed above and seek evidence of how such problems have been tackled in other organizations. For some leaders, going outside their organization means going beyond their comfort zone. Often they will say, 'Ah but it is different there, they don't have the problems we have.' Many leaders feel their situation or organization is unique; this is what I sometimes refer to as 'terminal uniqueness'. When encouraged to venture beyond their current organization, even sector, leaders often find surprising benefits. In a programme I was running with leaders in a financial services organization, they were facing challenges associated with managing change. They had a very traditional workforce, set in their ways and were under increasing pressure to innovate and to create a more dynamic culture. We were setting up a workshop to explore this theme and I was asked to help find an external contributor to join the workshop to stimulate thinking. I invited my friend Ian Barrington, the manager of a children's hospital. At first, the participants were skeptical as to whether there was anything a hospital manager could teach them in financial services. However, Ian spoke about his experience of managing the relocation of the hospital to a new facility, of how he had to deal with resistance from staff who had spent their whole career in one location, of how he used the challenge as an opportunity to create a new culture. Gradually, his talk turned into a very focused question and answer session and then a joint problem solving session as the finance sector leaders realized there were tremendous parallels they could draw on to inform their own role as leaders. Furthermore, they were about to manage a major relocation from their old offices to a dockside location; they ended up inviting Ian to join the steering group which was managing this process. So here was an organization actually less than a mile away that was tackling similar challenges in a different context that provided excellent ground for research in the form of comparison.

When conducting research into business problems, leaders should consider the process and methods they are using for their research. Again, talk of research methods may sound very academic to business people, but all organizations are using a range of research methods to investigate problems or assess priorities. For instance, an employee satisfaction survey involves the survey method of formulating questions, structuring them, identifying a target population, seeking responses and then analyzing these to come to some conclusions, resulting in some action. Hopefully, if the research was well conducted, then the analysis was good, the findings were valid and the decision making in terms of action was well judged. If so, there is likely to be business improvement. However, there are many pitfalls if such research is conducted in a slapdash way. The findings can easily become meaningless if for instance, the survey is poorly constructed, ignoring what is known about good survey design, if analysis of results is flawed, or if the person interpreting the results decides to put a spin on them to suit personal beliefs and self interest. So a leader as a researcher would do well to consider good practice in terms of their research methods, and there is much written about this and to be learnt from the academic world, once you cut through the language barrier. I recommend reading some good texts on research methods, in particular those that are concerned with what is often known as real world research.

One senior manager in a motor dealership was describing to me how she was working on a project to improve the customer experience when purchasing a car. She was intending to rely on data from a mystery shopper exercise. Why? Because they had been using the mystery shopper exercise as the main source of data to inform decision making about service improvement for years. When I probed into validity of the data coming from this method of research she said she knew it was flawed. Sales staff, she said, would work out within a few minutes they were being mystery shopped, and then would react in one of two ways. They would either over emphasize customer service behaviours or they would psychologically 'check-out' and just go through the motions of trying to make a sale. She realized this was leading to the provision and analysis of meaningless data that in no way reflected the real customer experience. I challenged her as a leader to implement a new improved method for researching the customer experience. She understood the point I was making, but was resistant to changing the mystery shopper process. She felt it was so well accepted as a method with too many people having a vested interested in it, that to suggest a different approach would be unpopular and meet with serious objections. As mentioned earlier, leadership is about being sensitive to the politics and sensitivities within the organizational context, so I felt she was right to acknowledge the history and viewpoints of key stakeholders. However, leadership is also about being courageous, daring to be different, and challenging the *status quo*.

RIH: *Before the 2000 expedition you did a lot of research. How did you go about this?*

AWC: I first used the Internet, then I read a lot of the reports and findings from the same sort of projects that had failed. I looked at the one thing that stopped them. I then went and met as many people as I could who had attempted it. I then went and lived with the Inuit Eskimos to understand how they live on the ice, how they read the ice, to test equipment. I did this for three years in a row. I wanted to research all I could on what we needed to get there. I turned a lot of the procedures other people had used on their heads. I changed the diets and I questioned everything. Changing the diet led to a new diet being recognized by the Greenwich Maritime museum as a short term modern Polar diet compared to the diets used by Amundsen and Captain Scott, so even against two iconic travellers. But the other thing we pioneered was the attitude of the team – we had to get the attitude in terms of being motivated right in the team to get the diet to work.

The traditional approach has been to take 60 percent fat in your diet, and at the end of the day you have to eat a pound of Indian ghee. I said if we can keep the motivation and the vision and the goals alive in our mind constantly and continually review and improve, rather than wait for a problem…if we can keep the attitude right, we can do this as a group and we don't need the fat. We needed the energy to keep the muscles moving. Diet just became the fuel in the car, a very practical diet, but you needed the right attitude to do this.

- On Self Belief -

RIH: Most of the leaders I deal with in the corporate world have not been leaders all their life. In fact for many of them leadership is a role that they have had thrust upon them, having risen from the ranks of professional functionary or technical specialist. Many, when they find themselves on a leadership development programme, are prepared to talk about other people as leaders, but when I ask them about themselves as leaders they become awkward and embarrassed. It is as though leadership is something external to them, and they cannot really see themselves as leaders. However, talk to people lower down the organizational hierarchy in the functions which they head, and you realize they very much are seen by others as the leaders.

This highlights for me the importance of self image. How you see yourself influences how you feel, and this influences how you behave. How you behave is interpreted by others and determines the impression others have of you. If they have a certain impression of you then they will behave in a certain way towards you. This confirms for you your view of yourself. Your initial thinking about yourself serves as self-fulfilling prophecy.

Most people rarely begin to exploit their true potential and often the reason for this is they hold self limiting beliefs about their own ability. Often you gain an insight to a person's self image when they make comments such as:

'That's just like me, screwing up the people side of things'

'I'm not sure I want to make that speech, it's just not me'

'I never have been so good at dealing with technology'

'Figures are my Achilles heel'

Limiting self beliefs are often reinforced by supposed 'experts'. These are the people who we allow to influence our feelings about ourselves. They may be parents, siblings, peers at work or bosses. The boss who says, 'let me take care of the business development side of things. You are stronger in terms of administration internally. I can see you are a little less comfortable dealing with the clients direct', may appear to be helpful and supportive. However, he or she may also be sowing seeds of doubt in your own mind about your own abilities. This is not always a conscious effort to undermine your confidence, but sometimes it is. By such making such a throwaway comment, it preys on your mind or serves to confirm a niggling self doubt that you have about your own capabilities. It reinforces the self belief that, 'I am not so good at business development and forming relationships with clients. I had better stick to what I am good at.'

This leads to the creation of a comfort zone within which you operate. If you have a belief about yourself that you are not so good in dealing with the clients then when the opportunity arises to lead a client visit, you may prefer to stay within your self limiting comfort zone. This is a form of avoidance and sometimes people can be very creative in how they avoid being pushed outside their comfort zone. For instance, on the day of the client visit you might arrange other activities for yourself, arrange to be off site or take a day's annual leave.

So the 'experts' are only experts in as much as we ascribe expertise to them. We allow them to infect our thinking. And more often we selectively notice the feedback coming from the negative experts. These are the people who will tell you more about what you cannot do than what you can, and what you will not achieve rather than what you will. When discussing this on leadership programmes, I often ask participants to list the positive and the negative experts in their life, past and present. I ask them to re-appraise whether they should continue to attach such value to what these people have said about them and allow it to influence their self-image, and therefore their feelings and behaviour. A key question is, 'How clearly are you seeing things?' When you look closely you may find there are positive experts who have belief in you but you have ignored them.

If you can form a realistic assessment of your own comfort zones based on your self image, and if you accept the view that by continuing to operate within your comfort zone, then you will fail to achieve your potential, how do you do something about it? Well, there are three strategies I want to describe for pushing back the comfort zone, for achieving new heights.

Flooding

Flooding is the technique where we move a long way outside of our comfort zone and literally get 'flooded' with the experience. For example, a gentle person who believes that they are not particularly good at confronting others, could be asked to represent the organization in a difficult confrontation with a difficult director who is known for her aggressive personal style.

Most of us will have experienced this sort of approach. It becomes a case of 'sink or swim.' Flooding is common approach used in many organizations and for many individuals this is a useful and expedient approach - they swim. Unfortunately, some people are not so lucky - they drown! Where this approach has been used unsuccessfully, then the impact on the individual is not only highly stressful but can also be catastrophic: the person may not try anything like it ever again.

Coaching

One way of developing effective behaviour and learning in others is to use techniques of coaching and encouragement. It is a more gradual approach than flooding, but it is a more reliable method and less risky. For example, to improve the ability of the novice tennis player, the coach would gradually encourage good tennis strokes by working through the following sort of procedure:

1   Explain the principles of how to hit the ball

2   Demonstrate to the trainee in stages how to do it

3   Watch the trainee doing it

4   Provide feedback on performance

5   Give encouragement

6   Allow time for practice

7   Observe improved performance and give further advice and encouragement.

Effective coaches will deal particularly well with stages 5 and 7 in this procedure; they will give encouragement which is appropriate considering the level of the coachee. This means that it is likely that a true novice will be given praise for efforts which, compared to the professional's own standards and abilities are actually relatively weak. Such encouragement is meant to instill confidence and persistence and as the novice starts to improve, so gradually the standard required to generate the amount of praise which was provided at the start, increases. The skill of the coach is to judge the current level of the trainee and therefore the correct positioning of feedback to develop optimum improvement. Gradually the coachee's performance is 'shaped' in the right direction.

Such an approach has been prevalent in many leadership development initiatives in recent years. Whether through the off-job training programme or the coaching provided on the job by the line manager, the emphasis has been placed on developing effective performance by breaking the desired task or skill down into component parts and then allowing time for practice and giving feedback and encouragement.

Desensitizing

Desensitizing is where the individual moves slowly, bit by bit outside their comfort zone. If we take the previous example of a person who is lacking in confidence in dealing with confrontation, you might start by allowing them to sit in on a meeting where another person is in the lead role. Then at a future meeting you involve them in a having minor role but they are participating. Then you allow them to take the lead. Gradually they become desensitized to the fear they held. Desensitizing is more likely than flooding to ensure success, but it can take a considerable period of time and still involves a level of applied risk taking by the learner.

Visualization

We can also move outside our comfort zones by managing our mental processes. What we do here is use in a positive way the fact that our thinking affects our feelings which in turn affects our behaviour. So by controlling our thinking, by imprinting positive images of success, we create such strong images in our subconscious that our behaviour falls in line with our thinking. This is the approach that successful sportsmen and women often use in order to create competitive edge. When all are fairly equal physically at the top of a sport, it is the ability to create a positive image of success which can give them the edge. We have used this approach with leaders in business, helping them to create a new self image and to challenge negative self images.

You might consider these questions in relation to yourself as a leader:

- What are the areas of your life where you have a positive self image?
- Where do you have less than positive self image?
- How has this self image been formed?
- How clearly are you seeing things?
- To what extent do you engage in negative self talk?
- Who are the 'experts' who have influenced your thinking about you?
- Should you continue to ascribe expertise to these people?

RIH: *For the 2000 Expedition - did it feel like a mission that was driving you, was there an inner drive?*

AWC: Yes, I think so – there are a lot of clichés like 'you are only on this earth for a short time.' I have never accepted being a bystander or accepting that 'this is it.' I have always felt there has to be more to life. This does mean I am non-conformist. It didn't always work out for me. I got busted three times in the Marines. But I take the view that unless you challenge things, nothing is going to change. If you are not going to challenge things. then you only have yourself to blame if you end up frustrated.

RIH: *How do you approach the preparation for major expeditions – is there a mental as well as physical side?*

AWC: Both the physical and mental sides need serious attention. The physical side of it is probably the easy side, it is practical, and there is a need for fitness, a commitment a sacrifice. But on the mental side, I think there is a natural tendency to take the path of least resistance. Until you have pushed yourself beyond what you see as your normal capabilities, I find myself saying 'why are you doing this again?' What drives me to keep doing it is constantly learning. I know the experience of the last trip gives me learning and I want to test this out by going further next time. I aim to get as much learning, technology and innovation behind me. There are lessons out on the ice which help in life generally; how to approach problems, the way you treat people, the way you look at adversity.

RIH: *What about your own level of self belief?*

AWC: If you were to ask what I believe in, what is my faith, I would say I believe in myself. It may sound arrogant but I don't mean to be.

RIH: *How do you allow other people to influence your own view of yourself, your level of confidence?*

AWC: I have read a lot about previous explorers and adventurers and have learnt a lot from history. I have learnt through my actions and by constantly reviewing and researching what I do. I don't see myself as a role model, though some senior business leaders have told me they have taken a lead from me. This was not my aim but it is good to realize this is a consequence of what I have done.

RIH: I had an interesting discussion over dinner with a middle manager, Andrew, who was on a leadership programme we were running with a major finance organization. He was tackling a Leadership Question relating to introducing changes to an existing process and had just earlier that day spent time at a very frustrating meeting. He said he had prepared well, had done his research, had compelling data to hand and really felt he was about to gain acceptance for his proposals at the meeting. The disappointment was that there was one senior manager at the meeting who scuppered his proposals but not by presenting any reasoned argument or logic. He had used emotional arguments, a loud voice and his seniority to dismiss the proposals, and other people in the meeting seemed to go along with him when he had made his feelings clear.

Andrew was asking what he had done wrong, feeling that he had played the game by the rules but things had not worked out. It was as though he was looking to me to come up with the answer, to identify the one thing he had perhaps forgotten to do. Instead, I asked him what he had learnt from this situation. After some discussion he realized that in tackling most situations in the business there would be a political dimension. Ignore it at your peril. He concluded that in future he would try to anticipate the political dynamics ahead of time, identify the 'terrorists' who would try to shoot his ideas down, the 'dark horses' who could surprise him when under pressure and the 'snake in the grass' who might spring up and strike with deadly venom. Equally, he would research who were his allies, would lobby them ahead of the meeting and then draw on their support during the meeting. Whilst Andrew had been in the organization for many years, and was by no means naïve, he had come to realize from his reflection on this event that he was operating in a world of practical social psychology and sociology.

Psychology and sociology are subjects which are taught on social science programmes, they often appear on management education programmes and there are significant bodies of knowledge based on a history of development of these subjects in academia. However, these are very practical subjects and we see evidence of this all around us constantly so long as people are working together in teams and organizations and pursuing their different objectives. Andrew did not need a 'class' in psychology or sociology, but he did benefit from being pointed to some of the research and literature on subjects such as emotional intelligence, group behaviour and conflict management. I believe this is the way that awareness of these subjects should be developed, through having a real business challenge and then looking to the body of knowledge as a source of practical guidance and support.

Good leaders are good practical psychologists and sociologists. They may not describe themselves as such but they learn how to influence people, how to motivate their teams and how to deal with the politics of group dynamics. In recent years the profession of psychology has strengthened its grip in the organizational or corporate world, sometimes I feel at the expense of helping leaders to develop their own capability as practical psychologists. Some organizations are even employing anthropologists and ethnographers to observe behaviours in organizations. I encourage leaders on development programmes to develop their awareness of these subjects with a view to improving for instance, self awareness, understanding of differences between people, of how people behave in groups and how to manage emotions more effectively. For many leaders who have developed a technical or professional career in areas other than the social sciences they discover another dimension to working life which can help them to become significantly more effective.

However, I believe many organizational leaders and managers fall into traps, often being seduced by the latest psychological profiling systems or psychometric instrument sold to them by a perceived expert. Typical of this are some of the emotional intelligence profiles and personality profiling systems, which if misused perpetuate a tendency to stereotype people, rather than see behaviour as contextual and subject to adaptation in different circumstances. If drawing on a personality based tool then I encourage managers to scratch beneath the surface and check the purpose for which an instrument was designed, what it is seeking to measure and what is its reliability and validity. Also, I feel in an action learning sense it is important to move beyond just measurement and assessment: there should be more focus on encouraging people to decide how practically they can use the feedback they receive from psychometric profiles. This means having a real leadership challenge or Leadership Question to address, which provides an opportunity to practise certain skills or to develop leadership capabilities.

RIH: *What is your view on how positive thinking influences outcomes?*

AWC: I say, 'never put your body where your mind has never been.' For me during the five years' training, every time we carried poles on a training run, at every step I would plant the left pole and say 'North' and the right one and say 'Pole'. I was constantly living it ahead of time, plus I knew the environment and I could visualize this as part of my preparation. I am a great believer in imprinting the image. On the trip we were sponsored by Johnnie Walker with their Keep Walking brand, which was so appropriate for us. I stuck copies of the Keep Walking logo wherever team members could see it, on the back of rucksacks, on the top of the inside of the tent, on the bottom of the teacups so whenever another team member took a sip you would have the message reinforced.

RIH: *You live in two very different worlds. How do you psychologically cope with this?*

AWC: You can call it a challenge. Some people come back from a successful arctic expedition with an ego but that didn't happen for me. I came back appreciating everything I have. It has grounded me a lot. The downside is that I only worry about really important things. I know I can move in and out of different worlds and this is what keeps it fresh to me.

RIH: *You talk about a battle with Mother Nature?*

AWC: About three quarters of the way through this was the way it felt, particularly when it was down to just the two of us – we were the only people on thousands of square miles of ice. We felt the only thing that would stop us would be Mother Nature – we felt we were battling with Mother Nature and having to overcome everything what was thrown at us. We concentrated on overcoming the obstacles that were put in our way. Even though we were behind pace, we did not do what others expected us to do, that is, to rush on. We would take time out and work out as many positive options as we could all the way through. The more options you have, the more chance you have of succeeding.

RIH: *What is your faith or view spiritually?*

AWC: That's a massive question really, what is your faith? You could say it was a rite of passage. As conceited as it sounds I believed in myself. I believed it was my destiny. Charlie was an absolute gem of a find to help me achieve the dream. I have no explanation for a lot of things that happened on the ice. Why would a lead open up or close up? Why would a piece of ice turn the right way to give us a break? We watched one lead close up whilst we were sat on the ice and it was as though it was meant to be to help us recover, to get us to slow down. The other side to this realistically is it could have gone the other way – but I do believe in the saying that 'you make your own luck'. We were constantly looking to improve.

- On Stress Management -

RIH: *How do you handle stress?*

AWC: There is the long term stress and for us it was the stress of knowing we were facing fixed adverse conditions. The project and the aim of completing it in 60 days was constantly in my mind, and was there until I finally stepped on the top of the world. So I had to break the project down into stages and tasks so that we could see that we were achieving results. For instance, we would complete a leg of the journey and then fold over and rip off the piece of the map showing the completed leg. To achieve a short-term target or a benchmark would relieve a certain amount of stress. Psychologically this enabled us to feel we had accomplished something and were making progress towards our overall goal. The long term chronic stress is part and parcel of the project and you can manage it by good planning and preparation.

A good leader also has to be able to manage the stress caused by setbacks. When we started to lose distance and looked at the overall big equation of distance versus food supplies, this of course caused stress. However, whereas some people would panic to make up the distance, we did the opposite. To manage the loss we put the tent up, made a hot drink and reviewed our plan. We would sleep on it and work out a sensible solution such as working an extra hour per day and work out the regain. We would not dwell on what had happened but accept it and work to put things right. Had we tied the sledges to our legs and run for a day we would have probably burned enough energy for a week. So to react in that way would have led to certain failure. This was based on wise advice we had received from Paddy George before we left the UK.

RIH: *How have you managed personal fears?*

AWC: I have identified all my psychological fears, such as I was afraid of heights. I didn't decide to climb a ladder to overcome the fear; I went and threw myself out of a plane and 150 miles per hour. I have done this all through my life. However, for the expedition projects I try to experience every situation we might face. I face up to the fear which are the risks . You need to embrace the fears and the risks. If you ignore them it is at your own peril. Doing your own personal research is key.

RIH: *You mention that you walked in the area where the Franklin expedition had foundered and where there was huge loss of life. Can you say more about this?*

Whilst training and developing some of the equipment and myself we undertook a three week manhaul over the Arctic Ocean from Resolute Bay to where the graves of the Franklin expedition are. It was a very eerie place and the coldest I have been. It was very special as there was a former Royal Marine buried there and we were the first Marines to return in over 150 years. They are buried on the beach at Beechey Island. As we approached the graves, a wind picked up and made a moving blanket of spooky snow and spindrift across the frozen ground. It was probably the coldest I have ever been in my life and frightening too with an estimated wind chill down to -70°C. It was a true survival situation but very daunting and a huge lesson in what the risk and dangers were of the project.

RIH: I was asked by a client organization to provide support for the training of the facilitators of some work projects that had been set up to provide learning opportunities for high potential business leaders. We ran the first workshop a few weeks after the project groups had been launched, on the basis that I wanted the facilitators to come along with some real issues or challenges they had faced. I wanted to use these real issues as the focus for discussion and development of the facilitators. One of the facilitators explained she was most frustrated by her experience as a facilitator. She felt she just could not get the commitment of the team, despite her best efforts. I asked her what she had done so far and she explained that she had held three meetings, but she felt some people were lacking in commitment, indeed some had failed to turn up. As I questioned her more I realized that she was referring to meetings that were virtual, held by telephone conference. I asked how many meetings had she held face-to-face. None. What hit me suddenly was the generation gap. I had been brought up to believe meetings were normally face-to-face and occasionally virtual. She had been brought up to believe meetings were mainly virtual, occasionally face-to-face. The point I made to her was that if she wanted to gain commitment to her team she needed to start at least by getting all the participants round the table so she could look them in the eye, communicate her vision and see how committed people were. She took the advice and came to the next workshop delighted that the 'technique' I had suggested, which to me seemed like common sense, had worked. This to me was evidence of one of the dangers of over reliance on technology. Yes, virtual meetings can save time and travel costs, and they have their place, but in order to lead you need to get close to the people you are leading. In order to inspire people with your vision, you need to be able to look into the whites of their eyes.

RIH: *How did you go about building a team for the 2000 expedition? I gather team members were geographically dispersed and this is something that business teams increasingly have to cope with?*

AWC: I communicated what I was offering, the positions available and a detailed description of the project and the outcomes. I communicated this electronically to a massive database and asked for volunteers. I could see the level of commitment from people's responses. A one line e-mail to me is not commitment. Some were prepared to write a letter, get in a car and come down to see me. Then I put together a questionnaire, considering if I was to apply, what would I expect to be asked. What qualities would I expect? I focused it more around people's experiences of events rather than qualifications, more about what they had done with their lives. I then interviewed and picked out two people I knew from the past who applied through the normal route. I invited others down to a day where I spent a very informal day with them and we got involved in various activities so I could see their behaviour and what they were prepared to do. We went running and got involved in various activities working together, and I was more concerned with attitudes and behaviours here rather than purely physical qualities.

RIH: *Were you working from a list of behaviours you were looking for?*

AWC: Rather than working from a list of behaviours I was working from my own intuition, having worked with teams for the last 20-odd years. I wanted people with a similar attitude and commitment to me. I knew the main thing which would make the expedition succeed or fail was the people, so getting this right was critical. For instance I did not want someone who was concerned to prove themselves as the number one skier. I didn't want someone who was going to go out ahead of the main group and leave others behind, which demotivates the rest of the team, even though he would feel he is blazing a trail. I didn't want people who were just out to impress others but in fact would separate the team.

Once we had the initial team selected I had to convey the fact they needed to show extra commitment above and beyond their current jobs. We spent six months training as a virtual team across England, Scotland and Wales before I actually selected the team to go on the ice, and decided who would be back at base camp, with very important roles managing for instance PR, equipment, and communications with the families, and relationships with the team on the ice. The base team were critical to our success; they were in effect working harder than us emotionally whilst we were working physically and operationally on the ice. It wasn't until four hours before we are due to fly that I picked the final ice team, even though we had been working together for six months.

RIH: *How did people cope with missing out on being with the walking party having put all this effort in beforehand?*

AWC: Some lost their places on the ice because I am a big believer in projects where everyone is up against it for budget or time. Some leaders start out by assuming people have to prove their commitment and that they are trustworthy. I started out with a different assumption. You have committed to the project as the first level of commitment so I place 100 percent trust in them. I assumed that those in the initial team were trustworthy and capable and if they lost their position that was down to them. For instance if someone was hiding a problem or not being entirely open this would eventually become apparent. This would chip away at the one hundred per cent trust and eventually they would lose their place on the ice. Or if they turned up late, or failed to admit they did not understand something, then this would count against them. The onus was on them to maintain the 100 percent trust they had won by getting through the initial selection.

RIH: *I understand you had a close friend who got through the initial training but failed to make it onto the ice team?*

AWC: Yes he was a close friend of ten years, a big strong guy, but he lost his place because he showed less commitment in the preparation stage than others. He showed a strong commitment, but not as strong as the others. I felt if he was losing the passion and commitment in the warm training environment then how could I expect him to perform on the ice? I put him in the base camp and I think actually he was relieved. Eventually he became the base camp manager and fulfilled a most important role, to which he was probably more suited. He managed any search and rescue, dealt with logistics, the sponsors and this let me focus on working with the ice team, managing and training and giving them my full attention. This took a massive load off me.

RIH: *I gather you involved all members of the team in taking a leadership role at different stages of the expedition?*

AWC: Yes, I think if the project is so challenging mentally and physically and you have total trust with the team, then it is possible for the leader to become a team member and for team members to take a lead role. You take the good times and the bad times together and the leader can become – and I did become – an integral team member. But you have to have the skills in place to identify where everyone is happy leading, or when they need to be led because they are nervy or lacking in confidence as certain situations occur. It was at these times I recognized I needed to step forward as the overall leader and lead from the front. I only led from the front 20 percent of the time though; the rest of the time I was an integral team member.

I think leaders have to exploit uncertainties, make more decisions and influence other people to come forward with creative ideas in terms of constantly improving things. They need to encourage ideas, and realize they don't need to give up control to do this. No one person knows the answer to everything.

I have seen some people who have tried to lead people in a very bullish manner and it does not work well. I have learnt from bad leaders. I also have learnt from people who have not been top leaders and have never had the opportunity to work at the top but they are very capable; it has been a privilege to work with these people.

RIH: *How have you managed failure? You talk about 1998 as a successful failure.*

AWC: The 1998 project failed because the attitude was wrong in the team. The dynamics were wrong, there were hidden agendas and these only emerged in the wrong context when it was all too late. This drives a wedge between team members. I was able to fix this in the 2000 expedition. I don't mind not being the number one leader. The main thing is I feel my opinion should be heard. The overall leader should be able to listen to contributions from all team members.

RIH: I believe the trend in leadership development in organizations will be away from the 'cohort' approach where groups are put through programmes in annual intakes. Programmes for leadership development will need to become more flexible in order to adapt to the different requirements of individuals. There will need to be flexibility in terms of when participants can join a programme, how long they join for and in terms of what aspects of leadership they focus on. There will be less standardization and processing of groups of employees. Programmes will be become more focused on real organizational issues, as the business comes to expect a return on its investment in people. Individuals will expect recognition and access to transportable accredited qualifications.

In terms of what Reg Revans called Programmed Knowledge (P) in the learning process, this will be delivered less in the classroom and more in smaller digestible chunks via different technologies and media. Learners will start to take more responsibility for their own development and realize the power of learning with and from others, rather than seeing learning as a competitive process.

As for the characteristics of leadership, I think there will be less focus on the model of the leader as a hero and more of an acceptance of leadership as a role that people can take on at all levels in an organization. This is not to say everyone in the organization should be assumed to have leadership abilities or potential as leaders, but for those organizations that make leadership development more widely available, they will reap the benefits with leaders emerging at different levels and contributing according to their personal strengths.

Currently there is a big emphasis on assessment in organizations, with wide use of, and sometimes misuse of, psychometric profiling. We have seen a strong emphasis on competency based approaches to defining leadership behaviours with performance management systems seeking to measure these and linking the measurements to reward systems. Some organizations are becoming disillusioned with an over emphasis on measurement. Where this is the case, the leaders and managers being assessed or conducting the assessments often collude to tick the boxes and complete the documentation without genuinely believing it is of value. Additionally, there has been an interest in recent years in subjects such as emotional intelligence and even spiritual intelligence in the context of leadership. It is difficult to predict where this will lead but I suspect there are an increasing number of mid-career leaders who will make personal decision to move out of direct corporate roles, but will continue to use their leadership skills by developing a portfolio of activities and occupations. Charles Handy predicted the emergence of the portfolio worker many years ago and I think it will be interesting to see how corporate organizations cope with the 'portfolio leaders'.

RIH: *Can you say a bit about your plans for a future Antarctic expedition?*

AWC: With the right level of support myself and Pete Goss the famous yachtsman, we have partnered with the UK Antarctic Heritage Trust in an attempt to help save Scott's, Shackleton's and Cook's huts. We want to do the same route as Scott and finish the footsteps of Scott. He is an iconic figure and no one in over 90 years has completed the same route. We will use modern technology and fibres because we believe Scott would want this: he was an innovator. We will raise money to save the huts, otherwise in a couple of years they will be gone. It is the equivalent of dragging a car from London to Rome and back, including going up and down 9,000 feet. A big challenge and we have been planning it for five years. We believe we can do it because of our approach. We have married our skills. Pete Goss is an incredible maritime round the world yachtsman. I have taken him to the North Pole and back and he has taken me to learn how to fly kites in Greenland and understand how the wind works.

RIH: *What is the legacy you want to leave?*

AWC: I have a positive view on this. I want to leave a positive legacy that I have gone out with a spirited heart to live the dream, but I have kept a balance in my life. And we have raised a lot of money for charity. We have raised over £3million for charities and there are things we have done quietly. You know in your heart what you have done.

RIH: *I understand you have a major vision for the Inuits?*

AWC: It has been a pipe dream ever since I went to research the North Pole. I went to stay in a tiny hamlet in the Northern Territories of Canada in an area of Resolute Bay. This is where base camp was for our expeditions. We were adopted by the Council of Inuits. I learnt a lot from them. One of the things which is very sad, is children get little opportunity to learn. They have as a community been taken from the ice and because they are so remote without government support, only one child leaving a school gets a job. All the others have nothing to do. There is no second chance for them. There are real problems with crime and drugs and alcohol. Their original culture has been axed. I want to build a network of internet cafes across the hamlets, and